A TEXAN AT BAY
By Paul Crume

Whatever you have to say about Texas, chances are it has already been said better by Paul Crume, leading Texan humorist and columnist for *The Dallas Morning News.* Here is a book about Texas in particular and America in general to delight every reader. *A Texan at Bay* is a civilized, slightly melancholy, and very funny lament for a time that has vanished, leaving mankind at the mercy of the modern world.

Paul Crume is funny, even when he is deadly serious. He is as tricky with tall tales as he is penetrating in his personal philosophies and comments on the social scene. And he is a masterful if somewhat sardonic observer of modern life, viewing with dismay the passing of almost forgotten virtues and the comforts of the houses that went with them. He is frightened by the endless onslaught of work-saving appliances and the constant slavery they demand. He mistrusts electronic banking brains, and he has never understood why scientists work so hard to make man obsolete. Full of middle-aged aches and longings, he re-creates the lost world of his boyhood on the West Texas plains, where he whiled away the time fishing for tarantulas,

its with
ing else
begin-
mayor
n.

ume is
oks in
rt, old-
front
earlier
smells

Crume
jaunty
atriot-
, New
skans,
gional
nining
style.
and
and
y-nine

tional
Post,
-aged
car,
umor
dotes
guage
tran-
scend regional boundaries and make the book rich in personal recollections and an engaging excursion in the most joyous kind of Americana.

PAUL CRUME

A TEXAN AT BAY

McGRAW-HILL BOOK COMPANY, INC.
NEW YORK   TORONTO   LONDON

A Texan at Bay

Library of Congress Catalog Card Number: 61-11126

First Edition

14840

To my father,
CHARLES E. CRUME,
and
all the old boys with
sand in their beards

FOREWORD

For nine years I have written a daily column in *The Dallas Morning News.* It began one day when the publisher, managing editor, and city editor came over to my desk and said "Write a column."

This is the way most great ideas come to people in the newspaper business.

As a Dallas column it was naturally called "Big D." The stranger who knows of the town's nickname at all will have learned it from Frank Loesser's bright song, but "Big D" was fifty years old when *The Most Happy Fella* opened. The term apparently came out of the cotton fields early in the century when the broad black lands around Dallas made it the world's largest inland cotton market, though it was then hardly more than a large country town.

Dallas was also the capital Saturday-night town for the field hands and inspired another expression. When the work was going well in the fields, the hands would yell out "We's walkin' to Dallas." A generation later, when football practices were going good at old Trinity University in Waxahachie, the players were still yelling "Now, we're walking to Dallas." Since then, the expression has died out.

On most days, "Big D" (the column) is given over to local anecdote and oddity. As a relief from the punch line, though, I have turned to the thumbnail essay once each week, usually on Monday.

The fine moral sentiments found in this book come from the Monday pieces.

They were meant to amuse people.

Paul Crume

CONTENTS

I

THE PIN-HEADED WOMAN IN THE SHADOWS

I was born in a log cabin in the Ozarks. Despite this promising start, it is as near as I ever came to the presidency. My first pet, the most amiable one I ever had, was a black-snake who lived under the cabin. He died in a flood of scalding water because my mother was jealous of his attentions to me. And though I am probably the only person now living who ever had a tree grow in his bedroom, I was never able to make it pay off like that woman did who had one grow in Brooklyn.

Our house in those years was an old one with wide plank floors, and the tree grew up through a knothole. This was in my personal room, and I used to lock myself in it for hours while reading, simultaneously, "Hamlet," Charlie Siringo's autobiography, the weekly dreadful on Old King Brady, and something called "Forty Years on the Plains and Mountains" by Will F. Drannan. I nurtured the tree carefully from the time it was a sprig above the floor. When it was about three feet high, I had to get a hatchet and cut it down because we were moving.

1

Our branch of the family seems to have stuck close to the American frontier as long as it lasted, not because anybody wanted to but because we couldn't get back. The family, at least our part of it, started from the eastern seaboard and worked westward as the crops failed. This accounts for my having once made an eleven-hundred-mile trip in a covered wagon and also for the fact that I spent the last half of my boyhood on the West Texas plains.

It was a comfort when some lady traced the family in America back to 1724. Obviously, the statute of limitations applies here. Actually, our ancestors seem mostly to have been honorable men. They were all fine horse-traders, and if none of them was ever President, they were all interesting. One of my great-grandfathers was a giant who died of pneumonia caught while cutting cordwood in his nineties. A distant cousin once fought an eagle barehanded. One uncle of my father had the knack of making a fortune quickly at almost anything he decided to do. He would then invest it all in a gold mine. Another of my great-uncles, a one-eyed man, went slightly haywire about farm machinery in the J. I. Case steam-tractor era and spent much of his substance trying to make the gadgets run.

The family has always been one of bold and original ideas. It has mined for gold in the Snyder reef oil country and dug for oil at Juneau, Alaska. About once every generation, one of its members decides that chicken ranching is the way to success, a theory that hasn't quite proved out yet. Our family has always been a hard-working family, and by digging many wells over the years has located more places where there isn't any water than any other.

My ancestors on the whole paid their taxes. They organized schools and argued bitterly over the truths revealed in the several hard-shelled religions. They fought in all the frontier wars, and in general behaved in a manner befitting pioneer citizens.

As for looks, my family has had to make do for some time now with the adage, handsome is as handsome does. Mine is a family that went out of focus three generations ago, and the only reason that the wedding picture of my father and mother turned out was that they were clamped into place for it.

At times, my newspaper has tried to break me gently on the public by printing my picture. This has never worked. Readers simply refuse to believe it's me. I have been introduced in person several times to some readers who still believe I am a practical joke being foisted off on them.

It is hard to explain. If the handsome, magnetic Crume countenance is one at which young women snigger, it also invariably causes day-old babies to laugh and dogs to wag their tails. It is true that my lithe frame, with important middle-aged additions, runs more to hide and hair than muscle. Most people have looked on it as did the Navy medical officer when I reported for World War II. He didn't bother to examine me. "You will just have to do the best you can with what you've got," he said. "They won't expect too much."

While my ancestors might not think too harshly of my career as a columnist, I suffer the lack of one family talent that would surely astound and disappoint them. I am unable to dream. Other people are always dreaming the most interesting adventures and telling me about them, but I almost never dream at all.

It *is* true that once or twice a year I have a dream that a pin-headed lady midget whose shoulders sit right down on her hips is chasing me with an upraised meat cleaver down dark, narrow corridors and up and down rickety stairs. Off somewhere is a faint glimmer of light, but I can never find it. When this dream turns up, it is something. The pin-headed lady is almost unbelievably fast, and able to turn like lightning. So far I have always managed to awake every time she has hemmed me up in a corner. I awake shaking and in a sweat.

I usually smoke a cigarette and think some great thoughts to get my nerves settled and then fall back for a session of sleep—only to have the chase pick up right in the corner where it left off. This goes on all night. I end it exhausted, and no wonder. I have run some of the fastest and crookedest hundred-yard dashes on record during those nights.

People have told me that I ought to see a psychiatrist about this midget lady, but I don't have time. She might catch up.

Anyhow, this is about the only dream I ever have; and if—while other people dream things that make them the way they want to be—I have to have somebody chasing me with a butcher's axe, I am not anxious to change things. Beggars can't be choosers.

My inability to dream is the stranger because I come from a family of great dreamers. As a child, I was thrown in with a lot of great-aunts who were very active at dreaming and enlivened nearly every breakfast with their adventures of the night before.

Aunt Abb was the funereal type of dreamer. "I dreamt Cousin Jane died," she would announce with a break in her voice as she took her place at the table. "I was there, and I saw her in her coffin. Lily-white she was, and so beautiful. Like a girl. Poor Jane." This was good for some loud clucks and white faces among the other aunts. Aunt Abby was the mainstay of the Western Union Telegraph Company for years, and none of her dreams ever panned out.

Aunt Mary was gentler and rosier in both her disposition and her dreams. She always dreamed of something like walking through avenues of hollyhocks and always met the most handsome and interesting people.

The most exasperating dreamer in the family was Uncle Mack, who was also the only member with any genius for finance. He was always accumulating a few hundred thousand dollars and then pitching the whole fortune into a search for some lost mine that he had dreamed about.

"I seen it," he would explode when the family remonstrated. "I seen it with my own eyes at the head of that horseshoe canyon."

It is good to report that Uncle Mack was cured finally, but it was after he had been the owner of some downtown Kansas City real estate then worth thousands and probably now worth millions and had sold it to put the money into an Alaskan gold mine because he had dreamed and *they* had told him to do it.

When the mine didn't pan out, he never doubted they existed, but he did figure that they were sneaks.

Probably they are. Certainly, the pin-headed lady is not an upright type. Sometimes, I have a feeling that I recognize her. I hope her name isn't Fate.

Everybody else gets the flu in the winter time when he doesn't have to explain it. I always get it when warm weather comes in the spring.

There is no explanation. It is true that thoughts of approaching lawn-mowing always cause a chill draft in my neighborhood. Anyhow, the world suddenly begins to taste like two-day-old root beer. I am suddenly more than ordinarily lightheaded. High fever gives a false feeling of warmth and coziness. The universe is filled with a faint whining sound. Voices that have no source call out in the mind. A hand motionless on the table starts an echo off somewhere.

It is all rather pointless. One could get the same effects from a cheap jag without anything like the trouble.

Medical science has not yet discovered this kind of flu so I have had to diagnose it myself. It is obviously Australian. There is no vaccine for the Australian Flu, which explains the professional disinterest in it. What is the use of discovering a disease for which there is no medicine?

After all, Asia had been around a long time, presumably with Asian Flu; but nobody paid any attention to it because it was of no earthly use to anybody until medical science developed an expensive vaccine required for its cure.

Before medical science progressed so far, we had plenty of cures for the flu and even the common cold. Nearly every generation has added something to the medicine kit of home remedies for such persistent undiscovered disorders.

One of my great-uncles, for instance, held to the theory that you could avoid all colds by eating hugely of black-eyed peas cooked until they had disintegrated into a mushy soup. We used to have Wool Fat and homemade white liniment. There was hot lemonade and soda, a nostrum that sometimes caused the patient to froth slightly at the mouth.

My grandmother's flu remedy was a big mustard plaster, the very mention of which could persuade anybody he didn't have much of a cold.

An uncle in the family carried on a kind of massive retaliation against colds. He treated them with a thing called the whiskey-and-aspirin sandwich. He would sit himself down and begin taking two aspirin tablets an hour. Between each dose he would hit himself with two or three slugs of straight bourbon whiskey. This went on until he would suddenly rise from the chair. His eyes would glaze slightly. The muscles in his neck would knot. Sweat would suddenly pop out on him by the gallon. He would get quickly into bed, roll up in blankets, and sweat the remainder of the night. He always got up the next morning cured.

My uncle was very proud of the remedy and once discussed it with the family physician, a sound man on snake-bites and accidents involving horses.

The doctor said he thought the remedy had some value.

"If you can get through it alive," he said, "it proves that you aren't going to die right quick."

A hot flannel rag soaked in kerosene is a fine cold or flu remedy, too. It transfers the head cold into the chest, besides searing the hide and cooking the vital juices inside the body.

My dad once warded off colds for the whole of a bad winter by munching on raw Bermuda onions. He warded off just about everything.

Fishermen are the world's wisest people. They begin each spring without hope.

Something about spring causes poets, fishermen, and gardeners to pop out like the japonica. Of poets, the less said the better. A genius is able to make a work of art out of the spring impulse, but the garden-variety poet merely loses control of himself.

The fisherman is driven by a sterner impulse. He knows that the cards are stacked against him and that at least five camp owners, bait sellers, and boat renters are now living off every fish now remaining in the United States. The fisherman pursues his sport out of some sense of the need for gallantry. He casts in the face of destiny. He acts well his part in the face of fate, knowing that no matter how large his catch, his balance sheet will always show money lost. It is significant that the early Christians called themselves fishers of souls. They didn't expect much luck but were determined to try.

It is different with gardeners. It is true that a Dallas

gardener starts planting every spring at the earliest possible moment, with the result that his plants will have plenty of time to die and get brown by midsummer. He does this, however, out of hope.

A while back, I bought a small house with some dirt around it and started to turn the back yard into the garden spot of the earth.

Until I had shoveled out shrub beds a thousand feet long and a foot deep, I did not know what I had been missing.

The main satisfaction in gardening is in bringing to fruit the products of the good earth. It is truly wonderful what beauty you can draw out of the good Dallas earth, especially if it is helped out by a mere three truckloads of manure, twenty-five hundred pounds of peat moss, five hundred pounds of commercial organic fertilizer, twenty-five pounds of iron sulphate, ten pounds of aluminum sulphate, four hundred pounds of ammonium sulphate, and a kind of liquid stuff which you can use to beat a plant over the head and make it grow if it gets obstinate.

Twenty-five or thirty truckloads of new dirt will also help the good Dallas earth.

"Let it be said of me," said Abraham Lincoln, "that I always plucked a thistle and planted a flower where I thought a flower would grow." In our neighborhood, we aren't so all-fired hot about pulling up a good thistle if it is growing.

A gardener lives in close communion with the eternal cycle of the seasons and the years. The flowers that wouldn't grow when you planted them last year come up this year in the bed where you were going to plant something else. There are also other things that keep the gardener humble before the wonders of nature. In the bed where plants won't grow, Bermuda grass will grow fine, whereas it has no taste for the soil in the middle of the yard where you planted grass. The rose you threw, in disgust, into a bed of old plasterboard burgeons with blossoms while those in the hard-worked beds sulk.

Still, it is all worth it. The true gardener learns a beautiful serenity of spirit. It is this, not twelve hours in the heat, that causes his blank stare. Gardening improves a man's vocabulary, inducing him to use simple, pungent Catonian speech of beautiful emotional coloring. It develops his muscle, the one he has to develop to stand bent over for hours on end.

Gardening increases a man's sense of values. He becomes fond of every one of his plants and will spend all his Sundays killing grasshoppers with a fly swatter to keep them from eating one of his leaves.

As a matter of fact, one is attacking our thistle right now.

It has long been noised about the neighborhood that I am an expert on insects. I have by now told all the neighbors except two or three. It is relatively easy to be the neighborhood expert on insects because there is very little competition.

A season or two ago, the wife called from the back yard where she was doing the yearly heavy spading. I put down the book I was reading and strolled out. She wanted me to kill a big fat cutworm that she had dug up.

"Do not kill the worms," I told her. "They aerate the soil."

Naturally, this law was passed rapidly around the neighborhood and cutworms were cherished. A few weeks later, the neighbors began lifting up their dead front lawns like doormats and discovering the cutworm cities under them.

Insect experting has not been quite the same, especially since the big beautiful moths I was zealously nurturing in the redbuds turned out to be the parents of a worm that strips leaves from trees.

It was last year, if memory is right, that I accidentally developed a new breed of grasshopper that spits tobacco.

The hoppers had descended on everything in swarms. In my yard, I was fighting them with nicotine sulphate, but they didn't seem to thin out much. I did notice that somebody had been spitting tobacco juice in all the flower beds, but I wouldn't have thought much about it if all the people roundabout hadn't started complaining about a tobacco-chewer who was making free with their beds, too.

The explanation turned out to be simple. Every morning the grasshoppers of the area were gathering on the foliage in my yard. They waited there, each with a visible case of the shakes, until I had done the morning dusting. After each hopper got his morning dose of nicotine, his nerves seemed to quiet down and he hopped off to his foraging.

It took an early freeze to stop the spread of this vile habit.

Some recent insect studies have turned up several new facts which I am glad to pass along. Some of them:

Beetles cannot possibly bite a human being, but some do.

Grasshoppers have hollow legs.

Ants are born spontaneously of the winy fumes from sugar confined in antproof cans.

Cockroaches are oversexed.

Wasps always build their nests on the tree limb you have just sawed off and are holding in your hand.

The true tree bug is just as bad as the untrue bug.

I have not had much to do with sports since the tandem formation and the center rush were confusing all opposition in football. It seems to me that the game of football has deteriorated steadily since the quarterback used to call signals by yelling out a string of numbers and then screaming *"Hike!"* The huddle has ruined the game because it gives the quarterback a chance to explain to the fullback what to do. In my day, the quarterback had to go back and point the fullback in the direction he was supposed to run. Spectators knew then where to look.

Players, even in high school, were less callow and inexperienced then. I remember a game at Olton in West Texas where our coach spotted a suspicious-looking character in the uniform of the other team.

He protested to the referee before the game.

"Well, what's wrong?" demanded the official, an Olton man.

"I don't know exactly," said the coach, "but he don't

look right. There is something darn funny about this."

After a while they figured out what was odd. That player was the only one on the two high school teams who didn't have a blue beard.

I have had only distant acquaintance with athletics since then, but I nevertheless end every football, baseball, or any other kind of sports season in a state of simple exhaustion. It just happens that I am a body-English spectator, and TV has given me too much to do. When a player so much as leans the wrong way in any sport, I instinctively go into a muscular strain to compensate for him. When a favorite halfback shoots in over tackle, he is not squirming anything like as hard as I am.

My stomach has grunted through more baskets than Slater Martin ever made for St. Louis, and for a week after a night when Hurricane Jackson used to fight I would have a neck crick.

I start each season in fine physical condition. I simply go stale before the end.

That Arkansas-Georgia Tech game of a season or two ago is a sample of what a man has to go through who conscientiously works at watching. In the first quarter, Tech was down on the Arkansas twenty. I had to stop one of those Tech halfbacks on a slant. After the play, I found I was balanced like a mobile on the big toe of the left foot. The right leg was thrust upward and outward. The left arm was downward in a vicious stiff-arm. The right fist was raised as a club.

Before the game was over, I had jumped up and down on the Tech quarterback. I had worked an Arkansas back

loose on a run through a broken field—and to do that, you
have to work your hips in a hula dance. I also charged in
on the Tech quarterback, leaped high in the air to block
a pass, and had to call time out after hitting the eight-
foot ceiling with my head.

My low opinion of skindiving started a year or two
ago when I read a book by Captain Cousteau. It advised
a swimmer who is attacked by a shark to duck down under
water and make faces at it. This is when I parted company
with Cousteau before we had even joined up. It reminds
me of the old cowman in Wayne Gard's "The Chisholm
Trail" who said the way to head a stampede was to bow
down facing the onrushing herd and flap your coattails
into the air.

No matter how many faces you make at a shark, you
are not going to look as ugly as he does. You can therefore
imagine in this situation who will be scaring whom.

Sharks are among the main things that stimulate my
nerves excessively. I used to fish occasionally on the Texas
coast with an old salt-water man, a former merchant sea-
man who became an oilman and sought the ocean out at
every opportunity for fun.

One day we were surf casting in water just up to our
armpits. Something kept shoving my feet, and finally I
caught a glimpse of a gliding shovel-nosed shadow about
seven feet long in the water below. I sounded an alarm and
sat for a moment on top of the water.

"It's nothing but a darned old shark," said the salt-water
man casually. "If he bothers you too much, kick him in

the nose."

I reminded him that another man a few days before had kicked a shark, and when his leg came out of the water there was no foot on it.

"Yeah," said the salt-water man, "but he missed."

It would be better to have a rattlesnake in your boots. Snakes can be charmed.

In my first encounter with a shark, I almost lost my life. It was a near thing. I was surf casting with Joe Murray, the advertising man. It was my first sea-fishing experience.

"There is a real big black bass on the hook," I told him.

He took a look and said, "You have caught a sand shark."

I started out of there on the run. Unfortunately, when you try to run in water, your feet do not keep up with your intentions. I fell under a big sea and took on some water. This went on and on, dozens of times, for fifty feet. Finally, more drowned than alive, I made the beach and pulled in the shark.

Then I killed all eighteen inches of him.

Four or five years ago I first noticed, standing before the bathroom mirror, that I seemed to be growing rapidly at the hips and belt line. At first it was a shock, but then the truth suddenly dawned. Obviously I was getting slightly astigmatic, and the whole thing was optical trickery. Comforted, I clothed my lissome form and continued on, as they say.

As the months passed, my astigmatism grew violently

worse, but who cared? At least, I was making an athletic appearance to other people. This state of mind lasted until I rode the elevator with the office boy one day. He turned on me a peculiar stare.

"Are you wearing your blocking pads today?" he asked.

It was bad to know that my youthful form was sagging, but I was thankful that, at least, I wasn't astigmatic. Everybody knows that the real sign of age is fading eyesight.

It is a mournful day for a man when people begin to call him egg-shaped instead of egg-headed, but since everything in every way is getting better, especially Russian missiles, there must be a reason.

Any man with the vast wisdom and ripened judgment that only forty years of living can give him knows that forty-plus people are superior to twenty-year-olds. Why, then, does the forty-year-old man break down in the middle like an old football?

I have studied the problem every morning, and ultimate truth has finally come out of the research. It is the enormous weight of the magnificent, well-stocked, over-developed forty-year-old brain that weighs down people at that time of life. The human body is not built to carry a brain of such proportions. Even when he sits, the forty-year-old must bear the weight of that brain on his hips. Naturally, they become overdeveloped. When the forty-year-old rises, his muscles have to lift the brain, and it is a terrific physical strain.

If you don't believe it, sit down and then try to rise suddenly. You will find that it is infinitely more tiring to lift your brain now than it was when you were twenty.

Blessed with this enormous brain and sharp eyes, I was willing to bear the cross of the hips.

It would be nice to be able to say that my own tribulations of the flesh had a happy ending, and they almost did.

About three months ago, my hips stopped growing. Almost overnight my waist shrank back to nothing. My figure became trim and lean. My chest bulged. Great knobs of muscle appeared on calves, thighs, and shoulders. All this was fine. It wasn't the reason I went to see the doctor. I had become mildly alarmed because one side of my face was hanging lower than the other.

"What is the matter with the face?" I asked the doc.

"Astigmatism," he told me.

In the last few months, people have begun to ask me whether there is any payola in the newspaper business. I am happy to report that there is, scads of it, very valuable.

I have just been sitting here and looking at the gigantic heap of loot that has piled up on the desk in the last few days. Here, for instance, is a box of slag from that diamond mine up in Arkansas. If you bust it up with a hammer and sift out the dust, you might find a diamond.

Here is a lead ingot, courtesy of C. E. Bassett, and five goathead burrs, courtesy of a gentleman who merely signs himself *Ha*. Alongside is a sack of genuine antique Bull Durham tobacco, very powdery and light as dust. There is a book, *Snowshoe Al's Bedtime Stories,* and a magazine entitled *Biological Contributions,* published by the University of Texas.

Here are also three unused horseshoe nails, mint condition, and one box of book matches from a charcoal steak house.

In the past, I have got even more valuable favors. A Midland stationer once gave me a real horsecollar. It was the workaday, canvas kind, not the fancy leather collar that a horse wears on Sunday.

I have a cigarette lighter from Chance Vought with these words engraved on it: *This Gratuity Did Not Influence Me One G.D. Bit.* I have a polished buckeye, a box of Bailey County sand, a wallet with a real estate man's ad stamped on it in gold, a Mescalero Apache arrow, a clip for holding sunglasses to an auto windshield visor, and an old pass to the State Fair of Texas.

Every New Year's Eve, almost, I get a can of black-eyed peas from the East Texas Chamber of Commerce, and once Deaf Smith County people sent me one of their potatoes.

In any mail, I am likely to get tricky new calendars, spare flashlight bulbs, samples of new menthol cigarettes, and petrified husks of horned frogs. Right after I have written something about green persimmons, I am likely to get four crates of green persimmons. Just now, I have opened a package and found a new kind of needle to inflate basketballs. The man is going to patent it.

With such gifts is the newspaper writer able to stretch his salary into luxury. So does the thoughtfulness of friends make his life ever more interesting.

Why should a newsman worry when he can roll in this kind of payola? After all, I haven't paid a grocery bill in three months. We are still eating off that giant squash.

One day last summer my managing editor came up to the desk with a look in his eyes as if he were thinking about something I wouldn't understand.

"Take a vacation," he ordered.

I pointed out to him that a man in my job didn't really need a vacation.

"The readers do," he replied.

When I finally rigged my tackle and went off for a restful period of fishing for tarantulas in West Texas, it seemed to create a sensation.

Actually, fishing for these big spiders has obvious advantages over fishing for fish. You put a wad of chewing gum on a twine string, find a tarantula hole on the prairie, and jiggle the gum up and down in it like a plumb bob. This makes the spider mad. He grabs hold. The hairs on his legs stick to the gum, and you yank him out. Some of them measure eight inches across. If you jab your fishhook at a fish, he can back off and move around it, but you have the tarantula in a corner. Also, fishing for tarantulas in West Texas has the advantage that there aren't any fish on the high plains.

It is sport of the finest sort. As a boy, I have often caught before breakfast, using a strong line and Wrigley's Spearmint, more tarantulas than I knew what to do with.

This last trip was a disappointment, though. It was somewhat disgusting to find that the West Texas tarantula grounds are about fished out. The few remaining tarantulas are too old and smart to clamp down on that wad of gum. They won't bite at all now unless you offer them an unchewed stick of gum, and about half the time they chew it up and spit it out.

I ran into an old planning file of mine the other day. Its contents brought back to me memories of many pleasant hours spent on company time planning assorted projects and adventures.

I never carried them out, of course. Amateur planning is not done for the future. It is done just for the planning.

A good amateur planner is always equipped with a stack of scratch paper and several sharp pencils. An idea hits him. He is ready in an instant to start planning it in detail. He writes down long lists of things to be done and things he will need to do them. He draws sketches of the way the project ought to be accomplished. His enthusiasm grows feverishly as he works and he finally rounds out a big, complete file, which he puts away to be consulted in the future.

My own cache included a plan for sailing the Caribbean in a ketch, thirty-four feet over-all, complete to menus for each meal, probable dockage fees at all the minor ports, lists of marine equipment needed (with note on what could probably be got secondhand at Galveston), and sketches of a new kind of reefing gear.

There was also an outline for a critical essay, never written, on the fetlock joints of Petty calendar girls. There was a plan for not getting frostbitten if lost alone near the South Pole. Another plan sketched out how to make thirty thousand dollars on the stock market over ten years, with exact lists of the stocks to be bought at which date. One sheet of paper, otherwise blank, was headed *What to Do in A-Bomb Attack.* I have also the big master plan for a book I was going to write on the tactics of ant warfare.

As you can see, this isn't planning for the future. It is a way of living up something in the present that you aren't going to get later on.

The one thing the amateur must avoid in his planning is any tie-in with reality. Some years ago I read an inspirational essay by Arnold Bennett, the Dr. Norman Vincent Peale of his day. He said planning is the art of using available means to attain some goal you had set for yourself. It sounded good, and I sharpened up the pencils.

"Now, what are my means?" I asked. The answer was too obvious.

I threw Arnold Bennett in the wastebasket and went ahead with a thick plan on scholarships to be set up if I ever hit it rich in uranium.

Occasionally some scientist sounds off on the idea that people from the field of science ought to help the government decide which of our scientific secrets ought to be kept secret.

From personal experience, after wrestling with several dozen science courses, I have decided that science is just naturally Top Secret.

It would not be quite right to say that years ago at the University of Texas I "took" physics from Dr. Paul Bonar. He still has them for all I know. I did study under him, though, and not only did he teach me physics but what he taught me has remained a secret to this day. No enemy agent has yet learned anything of value from what I was taught in that course.

The best way to handle a scientific secret is to teach it to everybody. The students to whom it is useful will know it; the others, if they are passed in the course, won't want to mention it for the rest of their lives.

Back when radar was Top Secret to anybody except Navy wives, I got a half-year's concentrated instruction in the stuff at Harvard from a man who might have invented it. At the end of six months, radar remained a Top Secret to me. For all I knew, the transistor had already been invented instead of waiting around until ten years later.

At the end of the course, the instructor had to write a comment on each student. He might have made some embarrassing remarks about my befuddlement, but he did the gracious thing.

"If captured," he wrote, "this man will not be a security risk."

I credit this unqualified recommendation with the appointment I later got as a Top Secret Control Officer. I got a bunch of Top Secret documents and a small but thick-walled safe. I couldn't understand the documents, and I was ordered to let no one see them. It turned out to be easy. I put the documents in the safe and forgot to get the combination before locking it. When I gave up the job a year later, nobody had ever asked to see anything.

I like to think that those Top Secrets are still the nation's best-kept classified information. Even the nation doesn't know it has them.

One thing still puzzles me. I used to think that the United States developed the atom bomb and handed over the secrets to the security risks. More and more, it turns out that the security risks developed the atom bomb and handed it over to the United States.

The longest journey I ever made, and the most memorable, I took on a summer day when I was six. On that day, my parents decided that I was old enough to walk by myself the three miles from our Ozark farm to the small village where my grandmother lived.

A small boy at large now on a highway could expect death at every curve, but the road I traveled was nearly deserted. It doglegged back and forth, following the edges of fields instead of section lines. I took to it with thunder in my heart and senses keen with excitement.

The iron-shod wagons and buggies had cut the dirt of the road into soft dust a foot deep. It was pleasantly hot to the skin of bare feet. A crow flapped its way across a nearby field without cawing. At one spot in a fencerow where blackberry vines grew, I was positive I heard the slither of snakes across the dusty grass.

I crossed the footlog over Long Creek. I stopped at a house farther on and talked with Mrs. Ed Jones. She gave me a dipper of water and asked whether my parents knew where I was. Assured they did, she said I was getting mighty big and brave to undertake such a journey alone.

Once a man named Clyde Tabor waved from his field, and once the Smith who was called Cussing Smith gave me a ride in his Model T, one of those old-time cars with tie rods that ran down from the windshield to the square front fenders. Cussing Smith was a fat little man with a beaming red face and white walrus moustaches. He was generally equated in the community with Sin and Whiskey, being a lawyer.

It was a long, wild, wonderful ride, and the half-mile of road flew beneath us like the wind before he turned off.

When I got to town, I found my grandmother absent. An uncle arrived, took charge of me, and informed me that she would be back next day from visiting some other relatives.

What seems odd is that she had been gone from home a week and my family, three miles away, knew less about it than a man in Dallas now knows about the plans of a friend in Washington. Only yesterday that was, and three miles was a world away. Now, they say, the moon is next door.

About twice a year I somehow get out of making a commencement address, and if I have to attend one as a listener, I try to send the speaker an anonymous letter beforehand pointing out that the class he is advising is going to furnish him at least one or two business competitors in a few years. This seems to cut down the supply of free advice and helpful tips and to shorten things all around.

The commencement speech is another one of those useless gadgets that bemuse Americans. I have been on the catching end of several commencements and can now remember nothing of what was said or who the speaker was. This goes for all of them except my grade-school commencement. The speaker at that one was an old-timer, a prominent cattleman and county commissioner of our precinct. He delivered a little lecture on the financial advantages of being morally four-square and ended up in a show of oratory.

"As you go down the great road of life," he said, "I want you kids to watch out for the cattleguards and always close the gates."

That was a fine and memorable commencement, the end of arithmetic forever.

My main quarrel with commencement speeches is that they do nothing to prepare a person for the great crises of life. You hear about always facing destiny with chin up and a stiff upper lip, because we fall to rise and every cloud has a silver lining. Nobody, though, prepared me for the day when my legs went out. I found out about this suddenly while sprinting up a hill with a full pack. The old legs would no longer carry me. This is an unnerving experience. It is a chilling first hint of mortality. When it happens, a man is inclined to sit down for a while and think on some deep philosophical subject such as *sic transit legs*.

No advice-giver ever readies a man for the fact that his own children grow up faster than he ever did, or that the life he had planned with the girl he married has got away from him somewhere between paying the bills, or that there are some times when he's going to be caught out for a day or two at a time without a cigarette in his pocket. These are the times that try men's souls.

Nevertheless, in commencement season, some must talk

and others listen, and you run into such things as a perfectly good credit manager telling a high school class solemnly that money isn't important.

I suspect that most commencement speakers are a little shamefaced. The reason is that every man knows in his heart he is pretty much of a failure, just as he hopes he has been a little of a success. Even if he has walked with kings and directed nations and been elected president of the Dad's Club besides, he knows that he has not done half as much as he could have if things somehow had been different.

This is the tragedy of man. There is no way in which he can mine more than a pittance of the riches inside him, and most of this immortal substance must go with him to the dust.

I can never get over the utterly improbable appearance that a human being presents. Consider the average man in his undershorts. There is his real measure. He stands stripped of his camouflage of pomposity and pretense. Look at his weak eyes. Note his puny biceps and triceps extensor. Notice his sour, unhealthy, buttermilk-color skin where the sun hasn't hit him. He has neither hair to guard him from the weather nor claw to protect himself. Under each sparse hair is dandruff; under each useless toe, toe itch.

Anybody could look at this miserable wretch and tell that he was going to do something sneaky like make an H-bomb.

Is this creature who matures only by growing around the middle and is unable to love himself before the morning mirror, is he the maker of dreams and myth? Is he the singer of songs, the tamer of fire, the master of the jet-stream and the ocean rivers? Imagine addressing the question to an impartial creature from some other universe!

Yet, man has comported himself well. The universe's greatest foul ball has behaved with debonair confidence as if he were not constantly brushing around the crushing toes of the gods. Too small to fight with the early denizens of the earth, he connived. Out of a gigantic and primordial inferiority complex, he invented. He gave himself importance. He invented things like the wheel, the cotton gin, and the curious notion that to be successful you must have ulcers.

The world was obviously fair when he came into it, so he invented the plow to scar its surfaces and prove who was boss. Were the rivers he drank from sweet? He showed them: he polluted them beyond all using. The world grew gray under his breath.

Gradually man has made himself superior to all the other animals. He only, for instance, walks erect and therefore has back pains and fallen arches. He only is able dimly to suspect that there is something wrong with his mind that makes him need a psychiatrist.

Yes, man is the unloveliest of the great apes and the most unpredictable. There is an honesty about the looks of a good chimpanzee like Henry out at the Dallas zoo. For what he is, he looks right.

Few other things on earth taste so good as the first half of a pipe of fine tobacco. About halfway through the pipe, though, an acrid edge smites the taste buds. Before long, the smoke tastes sour, strong, slightly moist. It is altogether a disappointment.

This is one of the things I have learned to take philosophically after all these years, and put it down as one of those great Natural Laws like the fact that you always run out of gasoline between filling stations. Man spends his existence wondering whether to walk back to the last station—or ahead to the next and call it Progress. Mere mortals cannot cope with these laws. They are the pattern of the Universe.

A natural law is something science has not figured out how to handle. Nobody has invented a pipe of tobacco with the bottom half left out. Nobody has yet invented a dictionary for people who can't spell and really need a dictionary. You would think that somebody could get together a dictionary listing the words you don't know how to spell according to the way you don't know how to spell them, but nobody has.

This pattern runs all through life. Left-hand oarlocks on boats do not push the boat as hard as right-hand oarlocks do. The tin whistle is always at the bottom of the box of Cracker Jacks. If you start out to walk straight without a compass or landmarks, you will walk in a circle. People go nuts in an election year and vote for the other candidate.

Solve one of these bedevilments of the human race and you will have blessed all mankind.

Of course, the human race makes some small gains in its struggle with the remorseless natural universe. Until a few years ago, one great natural law was that the atom was the smallest possible particle of elemental matter.

Another natural law was this: whatever goes up must come down. Human ingenuity has freed the cost of living from this old limitation.

Mostly, though, man is still at the mercy of Nature, who is sitting out there in space, smiling slyly, holding in one hand the world and its pitiful men and in the other a pigeon ready to drop.

A couple of years ago the British government had just succeeded in convincing the Labor opposition that it was absolutely safe for American planes to fly around over the islands carrying atom bombs. So what happened? The next day one of our Air Force planes lost an A-bomb and double-dribbled it all over the Carolinas.

It was the same one time when one of my uncles was trying to sell a wonderfully gentle old milk cow to a man who wanted a cow his wife could milk. Right while my uncle was declaiming on how the cow wouldn't hurt a fly, she let go with a kick that knocked him across the lot— the only kick of her career.

It is when a man opens his big mouth that he drives Nature to deliver one of these malicious blows. Most things that never could happen come off after the newspapers have run some headline about Man's Conquest over Nature.

I am convinced that Man is never going to conquer Nature. He may rip up and rebuild his own little world as he likes. He may have the illusion of Progress, but right when Man seems to be running the fastest, the sardonic giant will see that he busts his suspenders.

The best a man can do in this life is keep his mouth shut and his hand on his money pocket. Avoid such words

as *no, never, only,* and *greatest.* Clam up in the presence
of elephants, whales, and other stimulants of immoderate
expression.

Learn to dodge.

A curious thing about existence is how many men are
great adventurers without knowing it.

Take the man who has three kids coming up to college
age, a desk job, an unsatisfactory house on which he still
owes quite a bit of money, a pledge to the church that he
doesn't know how he will fill, and a credit rating at most
of the better stores. He regards himself as pedestrian and
entirely tied down. I have talked to them. I have talked to
old New York newspapermen and to farmers who are
temporarily going crazy watching the turkeys and to sales-
men peddling bolts.

Nearly all these men have had strange and dangerous
things happen to them, bizarre adventures worth retelling
which they persist in believing to be misadventures.

Years ago, in West Texas, I knew an old man, then
eighty, who had fought the Indians with MacKenzie. He
had trailed cattle north into Kansas and later into the
Panhandle. He had hunted cattle thieves. I used to try to
get him to describe these high adventures, and he always
did—in one sentence.

"Oh," he would say in his quavering voice, "it was
awful."

Similarly, the bookkeeper who ditched a fighter plane
off Guadalcanal is inclined now to laugh at his terror or
find it an embarrassment.

Almost nobody knows an adventure when he is in it. It

is an activity that is tiring, sweaty, and maybe plain ter-
rifying, and the sensible human reaction is to wish that
you didn't have anything to do with it. The odds are that
Magellan's men, when they finally touched foot on the
docks of home after that great voyage, remembered it as
thirst, scurvy, bewilderingly strange and deadly island
peoples, and the feel of the desperate last edge of hope.
They did not know it as a world-shaping event.

Drake may have enjoyed his roaming. Once his ship was
out of port, he had severed all lines of authority and was
himself king, but what of the grinding years on his men?
The great values of adventure are inhuman values. They
are risk, courage, and the knowledge of death and near
disaster.

That is adventure, and it is faced by each generation
in some way.

It is often said that all the earth is now explored. There
is no place for the adventurer to go, and still, in each generation, each acre of the earth must be explored again.
It is not the terrain that our grandfathers knew, and it is
not necessarily less dangerous.

And there are adventures of the soul. Let a man remember a dead friend and he will know that he has experienced
a person who had lived a strange and unique life that
never was before and never will be again.

We step unwittingly aboard the Golden Hind, and, unwittingly, leave her. It is not until years later that we
perceive what happened aboard.

A couple of years ago I visited a destroyer base and
found all the old Navy hands there astounded and faintly

scandalized. A retired reserve officer had died and, as was his right, had asked to be buried at sea.

This was bound to cause the Navy a great deal of trouble. In the first place, sailmakers are not easy to find any more. The destroyer men had to send to another base for a man who knew how to sew the corpse in its canvas cocoon and weight it properly. A ship then had to steam three hundred miles to sea for the burial, carrying not only the deceased and a chaplain but also grieving relatives. The whole thing was a trial to the Navy. It is almost impossible to make grieving relatives look regulation.

That wasn't what was disturbing the Navy folk, though. It was this: Why would any man of the high Naval type want to be buried at sea when he could be buried safely on land?

"It's not natural," said an old chief.

Actually, burial at sea is all too natural. It is the instinctive knowledge of this that causes a man to wallow in an emotional chop.

The knowledge that the sea forces upon man is always stark and always unsettling. Burial at sea is an act which says "This is the end of a man, of a name. There is no memory. There is no dust. Forget that he ever was."

It is knowledge to make wistful even those men who will not flinch. A man may know that it is true. He may know acutely how short a breath in the life of the universe was his whole life, and yet he cannot but hope that some small scratch that he put upon the limitless and titanic universe will last to show men of another day that he individually was here.

He builds himself a monument. He scratches his name and year upon a thousand Inscription Rocks. He buys a crypt or erects a headstone. He finds a dozen ways to shout "Hey, look, I was here, and here is the mark of me which lasts while all eternity drifts past." He does these things though he knows that his voice in the years beyond him will be no more than the echo of silence.

With its dead, the sea puts an end to this at once. ". . . Of his bones are coral made."

The need for a monument is the last of man's vanities. I like to think that the Navy man who asked to be buried at sea had simply shed himself of it, for monuments are a great clutter upon the living. They commonly carry on nothing of the spirit of the man they are to celebrate, and often they do little to remind the world of his name.

The faceless gravestones in the old cemetery near the Dallas city auditorium testify to their futility. So do the old downtown buildings that in obscure corners bear the names of pioneer hair-tonic manufacturers and carriage-makers but are now known merely as the location of some other man's store.

Great captains of men have cut their monuments into the pages of history. Others have made themselves a reasonably enduring monument in a poem, a painting, a story, or a bit of music.

Sooner or later, though, the Huns descend again on the relics of great commanders. Sooner or later, somebody burns the library at Alexandria.

THE CIRCULAR NATURE 2 OF PROGRESS

It would help one of these times when everybody is getting political as all get-out if either the Republicans or Democrats would promise to quit raising the American standard of living. For at least a hundred years both parties have been steadily raising the standard of living—and now nobody can afford it.

At our house, for instance, we have gone to great trouble to buy labor-saving devices for the wife—automatic washers, disposal units, and so on. We figured it up the other day; by actual count of the time it used to take to do these tasks, we have saved her thirty-seven hours a day. And what do we do with the thirty-seven hours? Well, the gadgets keep breaking down. They have to be fixed by other people keeping up the American standard of living. Ergo, the wife has to get outside work occasionally and even then her income won't cover the repair bills.

We just can't afford to have that much labor saved around our house.

Sometimes, about midnight, the notion occurs that the

American standard of living, like the dinosaur, is going to die off because of its size. Of course, the American standard of living *has* changed a lot of things as it has grown bigger and better.

To keep the automatic washer-dryer machines busy and make them pay, for instance, people need to have more clothes. When I was a child and shirts were boiled outdoors in an iron pot, a man would say "Where is my shirt?" He didn't mean *a* shirt. He meant *his* shirt, the one he commonly wore when he didn't have on the spare. One shirt was all he was entitled to get in that week's wash. Nowadays people demand a shirt every day and two on Sundays and the Fourth of July.

It sometimes seems that people nowadays have just as many unsolvable problems as they used to have. The trouble is that they have a better diet and don't die off quite as fast.

A few years ago, in our part of the world, people didn't get any vitamins. They ate dried beans, fried beef, boiled spuds, dried apricots, and even fresh butter—which, as you know, has no taste. The only way a man could get vitamins was by eating Spanish onions, and even then he didn't know it was the vitamins that gave him the lift. He thought it was the smell.

Then science invented the vitamin. People now are well fed. They eat properly balanced diets, and nearly everybody is too heavy. Between getting the money together to pay for a balanced diet and getting to the reducing salon or the sweat cabinet, the modern progressive citizen hardly has time to cook. Living the life of plenty is just about to run most Americans ragged.

The middle-aged man these days becomes a dead beat because he has to support this same American standard of living. It must be kept the highest in the world, or where are we in the race with Communism? Suppose the word got around that the American standard of living was based on frugality. How many people could you influence away from Communism with *that?*

The people who can really afford the American standard of living are too few to support it alone, and the nation still has some niggardly families who live within their incomes and refuse to carry their part of the load. It is left to the dead beat to shoulder, like Atlas, the crushing burden of American prestige and to uphold America's reputation for using things up.

Put everything on a solvent basis, and the mink-coat and yacht industries would be out of business. House-builders would have to limit their palaces to ones requiring payments no larger than the annual income of the average middle-aged man. People might start riding bicycles instead of autos, and the spoke industry would be halved. Everybody would lose his standard of living at once.

To the credit of American business, you can say that it tacitly recognizes that the dead beat is the key to prosperity, even though it refuses to admit as much in the full-page advertisements.

It knows that the man who saves his money and puts it in the bank is sabotaging the national prosperity and takes action against him by lending the money of people who have money because they didn't buy to the people who have no money but want to buy.

Somebody is always popping off on the theme that the government ought to handle its finances the same way a private citizen does. Actually the private citizen runs his finances about like the government does. He buys a house on credit. He buys a car on credit. He borrows to pay back what he borrowed before, gradually increasing his loan totals as he goes through life and the banks lift his credit ceiling for him. He is in hock until he dies, when the insurance company pays off his debts and clears the property for his wife. Meanwhile, he has had the use of a house and also the use of a car—when his teen-age son didn't have a date.

I am surprised, sometimes, that less affluent countries have failed to take advantage of our treadmill prosperity. It wouldn't be hard to think up advertisements for such a country if you were running it. "Look!" you could say, "No Standard of Living! Save your Money! Every Man a King!"

Unless things are changed, there may be a mass migration to have-not countries where life can be enjoyed.

A cursory look at any of the new-car models for the last five years will show you that they are hopelessly out of date. With the help of Allen Duckworth and Francis Raffetto, a couple of other Dallas auto designers with a reputation equal to my own, I have worked out an auto for modern conditions.

Consider the modern auto radiator to begin with. Our

auto of the future is going to have a little hole in the hood right above the radiator spout so you can fill the radiator without raising that heavy hood. We could put a little spout on it, and chromium-plate the spout, which would add to the dash of our automobile. We are even thinking of putting a little instrument with a dial on it right on top of the spout so you can read the actual water temperature without all that complicated wiring which today fouls up the dashboard gauge. As you can already begin to see, our startling changes merely simplify the auto, make it functional.

For instance, why take off the whole wheel of an auto when you have a flat? Why not have a rim on the wheel that slips off easily? See what the auto-makers are overlooking?

And why have power steering? Why not build an auto you can steer yourself?

There are other mistakes in the design of the present automobile. Nearly everybody has to bend down and squat to get into his car.

All this bending is hard on the back and on the tops of hard-crown hats. Why not build the auto so that one steps comfortably upward to get into it? Also, why should the rear-seat passenger ride with the top of his head pressing against the ceiling? Why not raise the top of the car until he has one-foot clearance? This would give the auto a lofty, majestic appearance instead of the cringing look it now has.

Once the auto is raised so that an adult can step into it casually, Mr. Duckworth advocates joining the rear and front fenders with a board, probably covered by rubber matting—a kind of step. Toward the rear of the step, a metal box could be mounted with a snap latch, a wonderful place to keep tools. Why have your pliers buried under luggage in the trunk?

On the opposite step, Mr. Raffetto thinks it might be possible to rig a kind of collapsible steel rack in which you could carry extra luggage.

There are bugs all through the power-plant design of autos as now built, of course. Everybody knows the trouble that comes from fuel pumps, cranky devices. We propose to solve this by the simple business of raising the gas tank so it will have gravity feed. And look at the average auto ignition system, a complicated business of miles of wiring, timers, points to burn up, and so on. We have solved and simplified all this by inventing a wonderful new device— the *coil*. You will start your car, as you do now, on a battery, but when it is going, you switch it over to a magneto. Tricky, eh?

We expect to have a prototype of our auto of the future made up soon, but it will not have a name. It will carry only a model number, like the Air Force's experimental fighters. We intend to call it the *Model T*.

A lot of jawing has been going on about whether nuclear explosions affect people's health. The whole argument is ridiculous. Of course they do.

The bomb was dropped on Hiroshima about the time I was thirty-five years old, and ever since I have noticed a gradual deterioration in health. I can't work as long in the yard as I used to. That darned radioactive dust has ruined the old wind. It has also messed up what used to be blinding speed, and I am no longer able to run the two-twenty in forty-four seconds.

The clincher, of course, is hair. After the Hiroshima blast, the survivors' hair fell out and lately mine has begun to do the same thing, in steadily increasing quantities. Several friends report the same symptom.

Cigarettes never caused lung cancer before science started nuclear fission. Nobody even claimed they did.

I had been feeling first-rate for years until in the summer of 1945 one day I was bothered with a ringing in the ears. It wasn't any surprise to hear the next day that they had touched off the big explosion over Japan. It takes a fairly loud sound to make me hear anything, much less a ringing.

After the first bomb test in the Pacific, my right foot went flat—not suddenly, but gradually as the poison in the atmosphere took effect. After the H-bomb burned up Eniwetok my right eye began to fail slowly, it being exposed more than my left to the prevailing winds sweeping in the strontium, and after one of the test series in Nevada, a boil appeared between the shoulderblades.

In the years before fission and fusion, my skin was smooth and fresh-looking after a shave. Now it is dry, parched, and wrinkled, clearly the product of radiation poisoning.

Lately, more alarming symptoms have appeared. Occasionally, for instance, I start to reach for something with my right hand and the left one comes out instead. This is evidently caused by some substance put into those clean bombs to make them clean, probably a detergent that has become radioactive.

The evidence that bomb blasts have affected health is undeniable. I can no longer get along on four hours of sleep. Fifteen or twenty years ago, I always had plenty of zip and drive, but since the bomb tests, I feel a little tired and draggy all the time. It has shown up in my appearance, too, and girls no longer spare a glance as they pass.

Altogether, the polluted atmosphere has just about ruined me. On account of it I doubt that I'll ever get back physically to what I was ten or fifteen years ago.

Everybody has been so busy lately getting excited about The Population Explosion that they have neglected the opposite and equal force, The Portland Cement Explosion.

Population may be growing so fast that we are running short of storks, but it is not growing as fast as pavement. Mr. David Cort, a splendid bellyacher, recently wrote a book in which he made the point that the U.S., in order to support the automobile, has now encased under pavement an area the size of the six New England states.

Everybody has known for a long time that within ten or twelve years the surface of the United States is going to consist wholly of (a) superhighways, (b) airports, and (c) man-made lakes held in place by dams.

When you realize this you can see that population, expanding or not, isn't really a problem. It will have to go someplace else.

A lot of people think that it is bad to hard-surface the

whole country just so that we can expand the drag race, but this is the unprogressive view.

I once shared it. I felt that all highways ought to be put in the Mojave Desert on the theory that people who were going to die by the auto ought to be willing to live by it. There seemed to be no reason why military installations and airports couldn't be put on waste land. You could even move all the dams to the Mojave Desert, though it would be hard to move the lakes.

It turned out that this was all wrong, though. I learned the desert land is not good for military installations. Something about the arid soil ruins rocket shoots.

The best kind of land for a military installation or a highway is good, deep, rich river-bottom land that grows a hundred or two hundred bushels of corn to the acre. Turn all this rich soil over and bury it under a ten-foot layer of crushed rock to hold it down and seal the whole thing over with concrete and you've got a *real* military base.

It is even better if there are eight or ten Indians on the land who don't want to leave and who have been made to check their bows and arrows with the U.S. marshal; the whole thing is perfect if there are three or four graveyards on the land that somebody doesn't want moved.

One big advantage of picking land this way for rocket bases, superhighways, and airstrips is that it advances The Over-all Government Program. Once we have got all our loam saved and encased in rock, for instance, we will have to start another big federal project. This one will build window boxes around on all the installations (even under viaducts) to grow food for the people. The day of the Federal Window-Box Project is all but on us. You can expect it to become a big issue in the next presidential campaign. All the candidates will be for the window-box project, too, though some of them will prefer it under private enterprise.

But one thing doesn't fit into The Over-all Government Program and ought to be abandoned. The government ought to quit building dams. They are mere temporary expedients. While it is true that all that water covers up a big slice of rich riverbottom land for a while, the dams eventually silt up and pretty soon you've got another big level plain of loam that you have to concrete all over again.

A single uncovered plain of loam like this saps the urgency of the Federal Window-Box Project. Any land valuable enough to cover over in the first place is worth covering over right.

A woman who works at our bank says the bank is putting in an electronic bookkeeping system and that everybody will be assigned a number. This number will govern all his bank transactions in the future. She says this will make everything more efficient.

Maybe so, but it beats me that a man who can't even remember his own street address will send all his money off with some number he has never seen before.

As for efficiency, the question arises *Efficient for whom?* The human brain already is beginning to reel with numbers, some of them with three digits. The average citizen has to remember where he lives. He has to remember his telephone number (home *and* office), his auto-tag number, his Social Security number, the number on his lock box, his postal zone number, the day of the month and the year, and his blood type. He has to remember his shoe size and hat size, various sizes that his wife wears for gift items, his wedding anniversary, and when he changed the oil.

With all these numbers and electronic banking, it will be no surprise if some bank deposit ends up credited to Voting Precinct 647.

As time goes by, I suspect more and more that all these numbers are a trick played by the mechanical brains to get people to do their work for them. The whole tribe of mechanical brains has become insufferably stuck-up and patronizing in recent years. They have come to look upon human beings as mere number caddies. The mechanical brain doesn't have anything like as good a memory as we have been told, but it has a gift for low conniving. It is not above calling everybody together and saying, "You remember this number, and *you* remember this one. Everybody takes a number. Then just feed them to me, boys, and I'll put them together."

A few mechanical brains working together, each assigning a human being a different number, could thus trick the human race into remembering all their numbers for them.

Luckily, evidence is beginning to come in that the mechanical brains, for all their lofty claims, can be had. Maybe you saw that story a while back about the man in that Eastern financial house who swindled the mechanical brain. His job was to serve up numbers for the brain to work with. After hours and on holidays he fed stuff into the machine that caused it to swear it had several thousand more dollars than it did. The darn-fool thing swallowed the scheme hook, line, and integer.

Man eventually will regain the upper hand from these monsters, and the time is not far away when each of us will have a mechanical brain to remember the numbers that we are to furnish other mechanical brains. It is best for the present to be wary, however. Not long ago a scientist in Massachusetts discovered that his mechanical brain had turned stubborn and was insidiously trying to dictate how he should go ahead with his work. The scientist managed to subdue the monster for the time, but there is no telling what fell thoughts are clicking away in that tin box unregistered on the dials even now.

Probably, the Things have ideas of taking over the earth and dominating man. My advice to the human race for the present is to go armed. Never step out of the house at night without a pair of pliers and a blowtorch.

A man named Robert B. Hincks of Dallas asked why the State of Texas, once it has had a man prove that he is over sixty and exempted him from paying the poll tax, makes him come in every year to prove again that he is over sixty. Mr. Hincks thought the State might suspect that one of these men is going to drop down below sixty again without notifying anybody.

Probably this has just grown out of a practice, indulged

in by all really mature civilizations, called Building the
Records. As you know, every really efficient corporation
has at least one man whose job it is continually to yank
other people off work and have them make reports, then
to raise Cain by letter when there are typographical errors
in the reports. In a year's time, a man who works assidu-
ously at this assignment can amass four or five new filing
cabinets full of neatly filled-in blank forms to show what a
good job he is doing.

As civilizations grow older, they go in for Building the
Records on a grand scale. You can fix when a civilization
became really mature by noting the date at which people
and businesses had to be moved into the streets to make
storage space for the records. This is an inflexible law.

The later Egyptian dynasties could build a pyramid but
were hard put to find enough space for their millions of
documents, and there is a valley in the interior of China
with no water, no life, nothing but drifting sand and the
occasional dust devils that dance across it. In cave after
cave in the surrounding hills there are records reaching
back thousands of years on the people who once lived
there. The people have vanished into the past, but the
birth of a calf a thousand years ago is immortalized.

The United States until recent years was a crude, un-
couth country where a storekeeper kept his records in
pencil in a pocket notebook and handed the debtor the
page when the amount was paid off. In recent years,
though, this country has become civilized fast, and the
national government is now having some trouble finding
enough warehouses to store the records in.

One Dallas man has a convincing argument that the moon is now lifeless because records crowded inhabitants off it. He confidently expects that our first expedition will find the interior of the moon stuffed with documents.

If his theory is correct, we had better stop worrying about the bomb and put our best brains to dressing up the files and making the individual records a little showier. A man of our day isn't likely to be remembered by his poems or his music or his crusades against the heathen but by his Social Security card.

Somebody came up with a little bit of information recently that keeps bothering me. It said that there are now more scientists at work in the world than ever worked in all human history before.

This is the kind of uncritical reporting that has got civilization in a mess. How do they know all these scientists are actually working? I know a Dallas physicist who carries a heavy brief case and makes a great show of getting to the office on time. He is such a brilliant mathematician that he will often take the square root of a telephone number while he is jotting it down.

I have had the chance to observe him at work, however. After he has punched the time clock, he goes into a little cubbyhole with a desk and shuts the door. Sometimes he writes down a number on a piece of paper. He fiddles with a slide rule and relights his pipe. Occasionally he draws something at a drawing board.

Nobody can tell me that this is work. There have been days when he hasn't invented a thing.

To my way of thinking, this is all to the good. I have a theory that as scientists work more and more, civilization is going to work less and less.

Even on its own grounds, or space, science is woefully inept. More and more it becomes obvious that science is practically beside itself.

As I read the reports, a South Atlantic rocket shoot a-while back proved that you can put up a radiation shield above the earth which makes the intercontinental ballistic missile useless. It is now necessary to develop some way to bust through the radiation shield so that we can use our ICBMs, which we haven't yet had time to develop fully.

In other words, all these things are useless against each other, but *we* have to do them or the Russians will. We have a crash program for ICBMs and undoubtedly will soon have one for radiation shields and radiation-shield busters, but science continues to pull out far ahead of its own reach. We don't even have time to develop the things that are useless, much less the things that are useful.

Sometimes I wonder whether Galileo should have invented the telescope in the first place, and now that we and the Russians can knock out each other's radio and radar, Marconi was pointless.

We have got into this pickle by putting everything to a use for which it wasn't intended.

You can put up a radiation shield only because the earth is a magnet, for instance. The radiation follows the lines of magnetic force, they say. Anybody who ever took high school physics knows the proper use of a magnetic field. You pour iron filings on a piece of paper above it and watch them rearrange themselves. If high school physics proves anything, it proves that if you use a magnet too much it will wear out. In the last year or two, the earth has been looking pretty tired to me.

Probably we have misused the ICBM the same way. Maybe it was supposed to stay on the launching pad. Now that the ICBM is obsolete, one would think that the manned bomber, guided under the radiation shield by a human intelligence, would be the wonder weapon of the future. They are developing rockets, however, that make hash out of manned bombers. With all this death in the skies, you would think that the future of military research would be in developing some machine that would crawl safely along the ground. But now they are making rockets which zero in on the heat these machines give off.

Obviously, the only safe way for a military force to travel in the future is afoot. This is what is called the March of Progress.

To the average, uneducated person, it seems pointless to invent something if you're going to turn around and make it worthless, but this has actually been the way of science all along.

By all accounts, that cotton gin Eli Whitney invented was wonderful. People got right enthusiastic about it. Yet, he hadn't more than got it going before other inventors went to work to make it obsolete.

They say eighty cents of every federal tax dollar goes into this kind of thing. If so, they wasted forty cents of my money in the last year alone.

There has been a lot of talk among our educators lately about developing what they call "the whole man," not just a fellow's brain. These educators can hardly be called progressive. They simply are not taking note of current findings. The trend is all away from "the whole man."

In fact, a couple of space doctors now say that man in the raw is not fitted for space travel. What they intend to do is chop him up almost 100 per cent and send out what is left.

For instance, they say his chest and lungs are waste space. He does not need oxygen. They can put a gadget on his wrist which will use solar power to cleanse his blood and do the other jobs lungs do. The doctors may have misread their discovery and have invented, instead of a space gadget, a preventative for lung cancer, but this is what they intended to do.

The space traveler does not have to eat, they say. They will cut off a hunk of him and bolt on a gadget which converts his body wastes into sustenance. He does not need eyes. He does not need ears. All we will need to send along of the original human animal is the brain and, presumably, the mouth. (Something is going to have to report back.)

Even the mind will have electric wires tapped in to give it the sensation of pleasure on the decades-long trip through the universal wastes, and it will have a cut-out thermocouple to make it sleep when it doesn't want to feel pleasure.

The doctors do not even call these products human beings. They are called *cygnots,* or some such name, and represent the first functionally machine-tooled man.

My first reaction to all this is that the project won't work. It has already been tried—out in West Texas during the long droughts. People dried themselves up. They didn't eat. They forgot what water looked like. All this did no good. They remained human beings even if sometimes they didn't look like it.

It seems to me that man has just about designed himself out of his place in the universe. The dinosaur's fatal limitation was his size and the quantity of fodder he required. The lungfish limited himself by adapting too easily to the brackish areas of the jungle.

Now man amputates himself away to establish a race of steel machines, each carrying a bit of human tissue and wandering back and forth from dismal planet to uninhabitable asteroid. Meanwhile the real rulers of his own pleasant earth, the insects, go about their business. The cicada sings. The bee idles a moment in the cup of the honeysuckle blossom.

They were hardly aware that he was around from the beginning.

All these scientists who worry because 75 per cent of some people who died were smokers are missing the point of the whole study. The key statistic here is that 100 per cent of the people die. This is what concerns me.

Personally, I have done everything I could to reverse this 100-per-cent trend. People die for a lot of reasons. Running the mile kills some. Others keel over from lifting too much weight after forty. People are killed by being thrown from horses. (This is the correct verb. No re-

spectable rider was ever *thrown*.) Some smoke themselves
to death. Some get into the wrong fist fights.

I have given up practically all these except smoking.
Having eliminated 90 per cent of the causes of death, I
still smoke.

I know a man who did quit. He didn't die, but after a
couple of weeks two people sitting next to him did. He is
now in the Huntsville penitentiary.

So far as I know, nobody ever argued that tobacco was
good for the human body. Of the two schools of thought
on smoking, one argues that people ought to quit tobacco.
The other preaches moderation.

The trouble is that all humanity is divided into these
two schools. Some people naturally smoke moderately.
They are born moderately and die moderately. They succeed or fail moderately. There is another type of man who
smokes like a coal-burner. He is capable of violently smoking or violently not smoking, but nothing in between. Try
to force the true immoderate into the shackles of moderation and he would blow a gasket.

Two elderly twin brothers out in the high dry of West
Texas illustrated this. One drank water all his life in moderation. The other wouldn't touch the stuff with a ten-
foot pole.

If an immoderate wants violently not to smoke, he ought
to go to the Big Bend country of Texas. It is the best place
in the world to quit tobacco.

A man thrown into the Big Bend country without tobacco has no place to buy any. It is too far to ride, walk, or
swim to a store that sells tobacco. In all this big country

there is nothing to smoke in place of tobacco after you have used up the buggy whip you hid in your boots.

Furthermore, it is safe for all concerned. When, after the first hour, you go mildly crazy, there is nothing in the neighborhood you can damage. If you get mad and want to throw rocks at things, there is nothing that you can hit. If you want to beat your head against something, the Chisos Mountains can stand it. You don't even have to gnaw off the ends of your fingers. Old dried yucca stalks will do as well.

Alaska is almost worthless as a place to quit tobacco. You can smoke spruce.

Maybe the best way to settle the whole tobacco argument is to allow the moderates to go on smoking moderately and let the immoderates either hate the stuff violently or kill themselves in their own personal smog.

And then let science get on with eliminating 100 per cent of the causes of death.

A cat named Jupiter belonging to Vera Lee Brown in Dallas brought a live scissortail into the house and laid it unharmed at Miss Brown's feet. It surprised her, but I know a number of cats who hunt constantly outdoors for mice and then bring them into the house and turn them loose.

What is happening is obvious. Cats, amiable animals, are getting worried about the barren look of the furnishings in our modern homes and are trying to recivilize us.

The decline of the world may not have started then, but I seem to have started taking a dark view toward it about the time the clawfoot standtable disappeared. Our homes since have become sterile, abstract landscapes in fitting with the world of atomic physics, which teaches us that what we see is not a cat but a collection of nonexistent particles called neutrons bound together with gigantic charges of electricity.

That is what has been wrong with the world ever since the invention of the atom. It is full of electricity.

I have had suspicions about electricity ever since, aged eleven, I was invited out of the audience to play straight man to a Tesla coil for a lecturer at the Lariat chautauqua.

After a handshake and a kindly disarming pat or two on the back, this lecturer turned mad scientist. He turned on his infernal machine, a great thing of coiled wires and knobs which spat blue flame and made a noise like the ripping of canvas. He then proceeded to do things like make a purple bolt of lightning jump from the machine to my ear and dance there, spitting all the while.

It was a thoroughly frightening experience, and before it was over almost every adult who suspected me of stealing his cherries or breaking his window felt he had got his money's worth.

At the end, the lecturer almost redeemed himself. He announced that he was going to stand under the machine and allow two million volts of electricity to pass through his body. It seemed to be stretching things a little for a man to electrocute himself to entertain people, but I had to admire his thoroughness.

I was right there, ready for this educational spectacle, but it didn't come off. The machine made a great noise and lots of sparks, but after it was over, the man stepped out unelectrocuted.

Which shows how unpredictable electricity is. And it is unnerving to realize that the stuffed animal on an ancestor's wall, which he thought was held together by thread, was actually held by a gigantic charge of electricity. Since Einstein invented the atom, I have found it impossible even to pick up a postage stamp without remembering that it is a delicately balanced, huge electric charge. It might go off.

The world of atomic physics is just a big loaded cigar.

THE SUBURBS
OF LARIAT

The suburbs of Lariat are numerous and well-populated: Amarillo, Dallas and El Paso, Lubbock, Clovis over in New Mexico, Copenhagen, Tokyo, Muleshoe—wherever any of the old boys have wandered taking with them the now-phantom world of those early prairie years and, one hopes, part of its wry cast of mind. More of its sons have gone to Rome to study music or New York to study painting than you would suppose.

Thirty years ago Lariat was a grain elevator on the Santa Fe tracks, a cotton gin, a combination filling station-store-post office and a small white church, with half a dozen nearby farmhouses for a residential section. On late autumn afternoons, the shadows of the buildings lay eastward across the vacant, flat land for half a mile like marks of blue powder on the gold of the grasslands and the kafir fields. In summer, gigantic lumps of cumuli hung over the flat lands like mountains of ice, and the distant mournful piping of the killdeer around the distant water tanks had the inner feel of a blessed peace. In spring the wind, laden with earth, blew and blew a mist of powdery dust; but the climate had its compensations. In all of recorded history for twenty years, we never had a tornado —or cyclone, as it was called in Lariat. We were bothered very often by giant dustdevils, but the cyclone came in only after people from the Midwest had begun to move in on the land.

It was a wonderful world for a boy.

There has been some confusion about where I grew up among people who don't know the plains country. Some say Farwell, some Lariat; but the question arises because of the difficulty of locating any place exactly on the high plains. In that flat country, the place where something happened and the place where it didn't happen look exactly alike. In the old days, the resident of a thickly settled plains county, where there were eight or ten houses, would direct visitors to his farm by routing them so many miles west of railroad distance marker 621. When the settlers first got up there, they used to place themselves as, say, twenty-five miles west of the tree. The tree was somewhere close to present-day Dimmitt.

Actually, Farwell and Lariat are suburbs of each other, and I did a lot of growing up in both places. Lariat is within spitting distance of Farwell when the wind is out of the northwest, and it was sometimes hard to get the horses stopped in time to hit one place or the other.

Lariat made the headlines during the Great Plains blizzard of 1956 when a Santa Fe passenger train was stalled there. As far as I know, this was the first passenger train that ever stopped. About thirty-five years ago, one almost did. The locomotive actually blew up right in the middle of Lariat; but the explosion hurled the boiler of the engine about two hundred yards, which was a hundred fifty beyond the city limits, and the rest of the train rolled on down the track into the rural areas. It left the town constable within his city limits staring at everything, a frustrated man without any jurisdiction over the worst catastrophe in the town's history.

Most of the time the passenger trains rolled on through Lariat so fast that the sack they threw off at the mail crane usually landed in Joe Robertson's cotton patch a few hundred feet down the track.

Historic events like a stalled passenger train have usually been more trouble than they were worth to ex-Lariat people. Lariat, being at the point where the Panhandle of Texas ends and the South Plains begin, is naturally the center of the West Texas area; but supercilious people, when they hear the name, begin to ask where it is. This is a stupid question. Lariat, Texas, is eleven miles northwest of Muleshoe, Texas. Such smart alecks deserve to be cut down as Uncle Hector Eton cut down a Kansas City hotel clerk many years ago. Uncle Hector, so called though he was nobody's uncle, had ridden the train with the cattle to the stockyards. He went into one of those big hotels and asked for room and board. The clerk looked at Uncle Hector's Sunday suit, which was dusty and hay-covered from feeding, and then looked at the name of the town on the register.

"Where is that?" he asked with a grin.

Uncle Hector fixed on him the glare warranted by such ignorance.

"Everybody knows where it is," he thundered. "It is on the far side of my south pasture."

It is not true that there was no activity in Lariat. People made their own activities in those days. For one thing, they knew how to observe a rain.

You are supposed to swim horses in it, of course. Anybody who ever came from Lariat knows this.

It was easy enough to enjoy a rainstorm then; you just seldom got the chance. A rainstorm always came with a lightning display. The thunder would shake the earth. Forked lightning would dance in all directions and the air would smell of blue smoke. We had a neighbor, a gaunt man with gigantic hairs in his ears and nose, who was a human storage battery of electricity. Touch him at any time and you would get shocked; during those electrical storms, he had a sweaty, dirt-cured hat that would glow with a light.

The main point in a rain, though, was swimming horses. A good hard rain was always enough to change the peaceful swale of grass that was Running Water Draw into a boiling, muddy river half a mile across. When this happened, an air of emergency sprang up in the towns along the banks of the draw like that around a big fire in a city. People hurried back and forth in pickup trucks getting men and boys and horses down to the banks of the draw.

Down there was a milling crowd. A lot of people would be rushing back and forth shouting important orders, and there would be much hallooing from one bank to the other. Riders, sometimes four or five at once, would swim horses back and forth across the flood.

The idea was that it was urgent to keep communications open between banks. Of course, there wasn't anything to communicate, but if it had been necessary the lines were open.

This never advanced the science of communications much, but it did teach a lot of people to swim a horse.

You walk a horse out into the water, and when he starts swimming, his hindquarters sink down, a very alarming experience if you can't swim—and the floods of Running Water Draw never lasted long enough for anyone to learn. The horse, however, always keeps the upper part of himself above water, and the thing to do is clamp down on the saddlehorn like a vise. The horse will carry you across. Some daredevils allowed the horse to drag them across by his tail.

Most of the horses were not exactly willing to swim, but a two-by-four scantling would aways invest them with an enthusiasm for it.

The men and boys of the community would work all day and far into the night keeping communications open. Women were kept away. They were likely to get in the way of the strenuous emergency routines; besides, every one of them had a habit of getting nervous whenever her son or husband rode a horse into the flood. Women were supposed to spend their day furnishing coffee and food.

All this made for a very pleasant rain.

In those days, we always made something of a cere-

mony at the end of a rain. At seven o'clock on the morning the sun reappeared, twenty or thirty men would gather
around the land office. The official rain measurer, a man
long on belly and short on breath, would disappear to the
back lot where he kept the rain gauge. He would return
in a few minutes and make a formal announcement of the
rainfall measurement.

The great event was then over and people could go back
to work.

In that land of little rain, a runaway team came along
oftener than a good flood. A runaway team was one of the
better amusements that our small town offered. I can still
remember how the town dropped prayerbook, bankbook,
and baby bottle and headed at a dead run for the scene
of a runaway. Citizens would race around the team yelling "Ho! Ho! Ho, boy!"—thereby stirring up the runaway
activity. The way to handle a runaway team is to yell
"Ho" at it and dash up at the horses' heads waving your
coat or hat, then quickly leap back out of danger.

This didn't have any effect on the team, but it gave the
whole community a chance to take part in the event instead of limiting it to the owner, who would be sprinting
at high speed, belly sucked in, a quarter of a mile behind
the runaways.

There was once in our family a giant stallion, a Per-
cheron, who liked to run away occasionally. A horse is a
person, not an animal, though he can't talk and write like
a human being and possibly he causes less damage. This
particular stallion was a great personal friend of my dad's

and used to follow him around like a dog. He was a good horse, although he generally took the attitude that he and my dad were equal partners in being bosses of creation and that neither of them was to be approached lightly by ordinary mortals.

Ordinarily he did his work well, even if he was rather cavalier in his treatment of other human beings. He was a horse of great personal force, though, and about twice a year he would whisper ideas into the ear of the placid gelding who teamed with him and suddenly away they would go.

You could fairly see the satanic grin on the face of that stallion as he cavorted back and forth before citizens waving hats, coats, and brooms at him. After rounding the town, wrecking a three-hundred-dollar wagon and tearing down a few fences and telephone poles, the team would draw up in a good close-order rank in front of the gate to the stable and wait to be fed.

This was the signal for Dad to get some trace chains or a tug and light into the stallion. It always seemed, however, that there was a chuckle beneath his anger and never any real heart in his punishment. The stallion never took offense.

The people of the town prized the stallion very highly, even though a runaway did not really rank with a fire.

There was no more light-hearted small plains town anywhere than one in which the business district had just burned up.

Whenever I happen to speculate about how I came by my fine manners and gentlemanly bearing, I am forced to give the credit to a burro named Pete. I learned the Burro Way of Life from him out there on the high baldies.

The burro is a stubborn, self-centered, contrary beast with a constant eye out for some other animal's food supply. If boys grew up with burros, they would understand human beings better. The top price for a young, well-fed, properly gentled burro in a town like Lariat was two dollars and a half. Nobody ever bothered to pay the astronomical price of two-fifty, however. The burros grew wild on the ranges south of town, on land that was too sorry to be broken up into farms—a country of rough, low sand dunes thatched with shinnery, wild plum and a rough, tall kind of grass.

Three or four times a year an expedition of boys would make up in town and head out for the range. Along with a homemade wagon drawn by two burros and piled high with blankets, skillets, and .22 rifles would be a couple of dozen boys, most of them mounted on burros, but a few rode ponies with saddles and all the other riding accouterments.

This expedition would be headed for the ranch country to trap a wild burro or two.

The burro is the fastest animal when wild and the slowest one in a bridle that has yet been created. When he is a captive, you can get a show of speed and insane anger out of him by gouging his withers with an iron spike (whips and spurs do no good), but in the wild state, in that broken and sandy country, a burro could easily outdistance a pony. Our only chance of catching one was to hide in whatever vegetation grew around a stock tank or waterhole and rope the wild burro as he came in to drink. The skill of any given boy in our crowd with a lariat was a great deal less than his own estimate. We were lucky if a four- or five-day camp netted one captured burro.

The captive would be tied behind the wagon and dragged back to town. Most of the time he had all four hooves set forward so that he was dragged like a sled.

Once back in town, the breaking process began. The first thing to do was ear the burro down. The burro is admirably fitted with appendages for this. You buckled a surcingle around him; a saddle would slip over his barely noticeable withers. You helped a boy aboard his back and let the ears go.

The wild burro is the most ferocious bucker, for its size, nature has created. He can jump straight up in the air with lightning speed, switch ends in one jump, whipping his head one way and his rump another. At the height of that one jump, the twelve-year-old rider would always go sailing spreadeagled through the air, but this did the burro no good. While one rider was landing with a whump and a groan, another would be climbing aboard. Fifteen or twenty boys would await their turns, lined up as if to march into a schoolroom. When one was thrown, he took his place at the foot of the line; the supply of riders was continuous.

After a day of this round-robin kind of battling, the burro would give up. This did not mean that he had been gentled. He had merely learned sense enough to wait until you were bent over before biting a walnut-sized chunk out of your hip pocket.

Old Pete had been through all this years before.

Pete was small, sleek, rheumy-eyed, wizen-faced, age-less and agile, though he had certainly reached the age of fifteen. He was no tamer than any other burro, but he was a great favorite with parents because he had learned a tolerance of very small children, those who could not hurt him. You could seat a three-year-old on him and come back hours later to find Pete contentedly grazing within a few feet of the spot where you had left him, though the three-year-old would be squalling loudly and beating Pete's sides with his heels.

The three-year-old could safely drag on Pete's tail, too, and kick his shins. On a February day when the air was warm, you would often find Pete asleep on his side with his small rider sleeping on the leeward side, nestled up against Pete's chest and forelegs and using Pete's chest as a pillow.

Pete's eventual downfall was the fact that he was a nat-ural safe-cracker. Locked behind that stubborn forehead was a knowledge of how to undo all the latches people put on gates and, especially, feed bins. When the kids grew up and Pete served little purpose, he became a pest. It wasn't that my dad minded that Pete could work the latch to the feed room. Pete always ate just what he needed, which wasn't much, and wasted nothing. But the idiot cows and the Clydesdales would come in behind him and bloat themselves. This wouldn't do.

The old man began to try to sell Pete to itinerant horse-traders. Two or three times a year for three years he sold Pete for a dollar seventy-five to one of these wanderers.

Each time, two days to three weeks after the sale, Pete would turn up in the feed lot. The gate would be open, and something would be down with the bloat.

Once Pete was gone two months. It turned out that he had made his break near Lubbock, a hundred miles away. My dad offered to restore the mule the next time that trader came by, but the trader was against it.

"No thanks," he said. "The lesson was worth a dollar seventy-five."

Pete later found a home again with another family with small boys.

We had one sure way of making real money. Any boy who chanced upon the bleached skeleton of a horse or cow knew that he could make real money, maybe even twenty-five or thirty cents, by getting the bones down to Mapes Produce & Eggs. This had to be done before any large number of other kids discovered the treasure-trove and carried it off piecemeal; Mr. Mapes bought by weight, not by the piece, and it was not much good trying to run in any chalky rocks. For him to pay out you had to have whole skeletons.

The discoverer solved this by cutting enough of his pals in on the treasure to guard it while he spent an afternoon trundling the bones to market in one of those red wagons that boys still use. With so many helpers to reward, the discoverer usually wasted his treasure immediately in such high living as walnut-sirup sundaes.

The bones were latter shipped out by railroad. It was our understanding that they were used to make fertilizer.

A great deal of fertilizer now is pulled right out of the air, but everybody in the old days knew that it was made out of dead things. Its ugly gray color was the color of evil.

At one time on the plains, bone-gathering was a professional matter. The late Frank Bryan, a connoisseur of such knowledge, claimed that buffalo bones from one heap near the present site of Muleshoe were shipped out by the trainload. It destroyed, he said, a plains landmark noted in the accounts of Coronado's travels. As a trade, bone-collecting was dying out, though Uncle Ike Osborn still worked at it when I was a boy. He was a shriveled bachelor who lived alone with a bed, a dog, a small Royal Oak stove, and a single-barrel shotgun in a tiny two-room shack a couple of miles from town. He worked around a little in return for eggs, a quarter of beef, or milk for a month or so.

Bones were Uncle Ike's cash crop. He was said to know the location of every dead animal in the township, when it had died, and when its bones would probably be ready for harvest. He was wise in the way of buzzards. He kept a sly watch on the movements of veterinarians.

Uncle Ike bounced around from boneheap to boneheap in a light wagon built on old buggy running gear. It was drawn by a horse so old and bony that Uncle Ike was accused of keeping a death watch on him.

It is nice to have clean fertilizer, but it is sad to think that the days of treasure-trove, even of bone, have vanished. To find an oil fortune now, you have to have geophysical crews that cost a fortune. You can't just go out and find a chunk of uranium that will make you rich beyond dreams. You have to invest thousands of dollars in equipment.

You can't even buy oysters in the shell any longer on the chance of finding inside one a pearl, which anybody knows will make your fortune for life. No, you buy oysters quick-frozen now. The privileged classes have taken all the pearls out of them.

Half the barns on the plains countryside used to be hidden of a Sunday afternoon in great, billowing clouds of blue smoke which indicated that the youngsters, theoretically without the knowledge of the adults who were watching the smoke, were practicing up on cigarette smoking. They were practicing with cedar bark. You got the cedar bark substitute for tobacco by stripping it off new fenceposts. It was long, straggly stuff, and the cigarette you rolled had to be about a foot long and as large around as a softball bat. No question about it, though— it smoked.

Nobody ever claimed that these were thinking men's cigarettes. When you had hold of one, you didn't have time to think. They were wrapped with old newspaper pages or full pages from the *Saturday Evening Post*. The magazine paper imparted a fine flavor of old burning rags to the stinging fumes of the cedar, and forever after tobacco smoke would taste a little bit thin.

When all the cedar fenceposts had been stripped pretty clean, there were other substitutes for burley. Most youngsters have smoked coffee at one time or another because, after all, it looks like tobacco. Coffee tends to run out the end of your cigarette if you duck your head while smoking. You can smoke it very well if you tilt your head back so that the burning end of the cigarette is always up— if you also tightly clamp the other end in your teeth to stop the whole cigarette from flowing into your mouth, fire and all. After a few minutes of smoking coffee, you feel seared inside right down to your ankles.

Cape Caperton, a friend of mine, smoked dried grapevine. It was so free and easy on the draw, he says, that you had to duck after each puff to escape the acetylene-like torch of flame that stabbed at your mouth. He says that you can also smoke crushed cotton leaves and that, when you do, you notice it.

I never tried either of these. I have, however, smoked buggy whip. This produces a very good smoking tobacco because, if you chop the whip into proper lengths, it is almost the same shape as a cigarette. Buggy whip tastes a lot like filters; it doesn't taste.

Cornsilk was supposed to be a good cigarette filler, but I never cared much for it. At times, desperate for something to smoke, I have puffed at dried prairie grass. You have to work pretty hard to keep the fire alive, and you can't taste much smoke, but I managed it.

After all, if a man has to smoke, he can manage it somehow.

Once somebody anchored a cable at the top of seventy-foot cliffs overlooking the Brazos. The other end of the cable was made fast to a cottonwood tree on the river. There was an old well pulley on the cable, and you could take hold of it and sail out over space as you rode the pulley down. The trick was to know the exact moment to start swinging your body from side to side so that you would avoid a direct, high-velocity collision with the cottonwood.

Every day a couple or so old cowboys would ride by and eye the contraption cautiously.

"Back you out of riding down on that thing," one would say.

Since nobody was ever backed out of doing anything, they would both ride down the cable, and six or eight people went to the hospital within a month's time, thus raising the morale of the community.

I have known some highly interesting things to develop because somebody backed somebody else out of doing something.

A small circus once visited town. Its attractions were mainly one midget who performed on the trampoline and one ancient and very wise elephant. A half-dozen Lariat kids had been offered free passes in return for helping raise the tents and carrying water. The elephant was strolling around unattended, pushing animal cages into their sites around the tent by butting them with his forehead. Occasionally he would go over absent-mindedly and get himself a snootful of water from a big tub, which we had to keep filled. He would squirt it around and otherwise refresh himself.

A certain boy who now owns a drug chain refused to be backed out of dumping about a gallon of turpentine from the sign wagon into the elephant's water. When the

elephant sleepily got his next snootful, he turned kind of electric, went into a sulk and made strangling sounds. At the performance that night, he refused even to put his feet up on the tub, and the trainer got afraid to put his head under the elephant's foot.

The midget could have saved the evening, but it turned out that someone had been backed out of loosening the ties on the trampoline. When the midget made his first back flip, all kinds of things tore loose.

Next morning the circus owner pulled stakes and got out. He said some hard things about the town, and they were resented by the chamber of commerce.

The plains country is natural kite-flying country, but generally we bothered with kites only in the spring. After putting one up in those March and April winds, you could tie the string to a fencepost and wouldn't have to service the kite again for thirty days.

The kite-building expert of the town then was a boy named Ethelbert Tabor. He was a huge lout of a fifth-grader, a mean and dirty fighter. Though he was tremendously strong by the standards of the other fifth-grade boys, his mother insisted on looking upon him as a frail victim of asthma. After Ethelbert had picked a fight and smashed some kid's nose, Mrs. Tabor was sure to turn up railing at the other boy's mother for allowing her brat to jump on an asthmatic cripple.

Such was his reputation that Ethelbert was the only boy in school who didn't have a nickname. He was never called Bert, and he darn sure was never called Ethel.

Ethelbert's asthma would flare up on him every year about the time the March and April winds were at their height. Noon of any day might bring a note from Mrs. Tabor asking the principal to excuse Ethelbert for the afternoon because his asthma was worse.

The Tabors lived right across the street from the school. Through the afternoon, the rest of the fifth-graders would watch Ethelbert treat his asthma as he flew his kite.

He had long since graduated from ordinary kites and flew only big box kites that he had built himself—huge, graceful floaters with a fine sharp response to each delicate adjustment that he made to the bridle. Once in a while Ethelbert would haul down the kite and take it back to a small shop behind the house for some fining down.

This never seemed to bother the principal. Probably he had decided that this flouting of school was preferable to an encounter with Mrs. Tabor. It didn't bother Mrs. Tabor either. She was already on record as saying that a person with asthma just didn't have the strength to learn arithmetic.

Along toward the end of one kite season, Ethelbert suddenly had asthma for a week running. Toward the end of a sunny day he dragged into view a really monumental box kite at least twelve feet long.

This kite's framing was of two-by-fours and wire clothesline. Its fabric was eight-ounce canvas. Ethelbert had accumulated a big coil of sash cord to fly it with. He proposed to launch the kite by getting a dozen fifth-graders under each side to hold it on their shoulders and run while he pulled at the cord.

It turned out to be the original American space machine: it didn't get off the ground. It was too heavy to carry at a trot. We tried to launch it by tying it to a Model T and heading into a sixty-mile-an-hour wind, but a Model T wouldn't run very well into a sixty-mile-an-hour wind.

When he finally saw that he had failed, Ethelbert dragged the kite into his back yard and left it. The Tabors moved not long after that, and the kite remained there several months, while the canvas became tatters and the timbers warped.

I never saw Ethelbert again. They say he later bought an airplane.

W. W. Vinyard was the Santa Fe agent at Farwell, Texas, and Texico, N.M. When Mr. Vinyard said something, people listened. He had the habit of knowing what he was talking about. He even knew who broke the top of his rolltop desk while wrestling with the apprentice telegraph operator, even though I personally propped up the broken part so that it didn't show until the end of the desk came off in Mr. Vinyard's hand a week later.

I spent some of my early years as Western Union messenger out of his railroad station. Those were the years when the telegram was the symbol of death or high business indeed. Ordinary people used to wake up sometimes in the night and lie awake for hours worrying that they might get a telegram. My duties were to run the messages, clean and fill the semaphore lantern, and sleep most of the day in the mail car under the station archway. I netted twenty dollars a month clear profit from this and usually owed Claude Rose and Leroy Faville, the local soda fountain barkeeps, twenty dollars and a quarter.

Mr. Vinyard was one of a collection of adults who grimly endured my growing up and prevented the growth of juvenile delinquency simply by not telling about it. Just by being the picture of decent rectitude without even realizing it, he became perhaps the greatest moral influence of my life. He was even a great deal more of a moral influence than the prisoners at the county jail, and they had a great influence for the good among the brats of my set.

The county jail was a small brick building that stood behind the county courthouse. Except with unusual prisoners, it was the practice of the jailer to unlock the jail each morning and let the prisoners spend the day in the air outside and hit a few licks on the postage stamp lawn. It was understood that none of the prisoners would be so dishonorable as to escape.

Once we did have an Amarillo smartie who was left in jail alone all through a Sunday, probably because the jailer was out of town having Sunday dinner. Out of pure boredom, perhaps, the prisoner knocked the back end out of the jail and ran off. If there had been other prisoners, they would have looked on him as a low character.

The small boys of the town and the prisoners were on first-name terms always.

Naturally, there wasn't too much work to be done by the many hands on that lawn, and you would usually find the prisoners sitting on the grass in a little group off to themselves—as befitted social lepers. Around them was a circle of the town kids. They came, for one thing, because the jail always had in it an expert with the guitar or Jew's harp. I remember one bony, tall guitarist who could sing "Prison bars all around me, guard a-pacin' by the door" and weep to himself though the door to his jail was obviously wide open. Also, the jail held men with wondrous life stories that were the nearest thing in the prairie country to the Arabian Nights, and all with a moral ending.

On that semifrontier we probably had a higher grade of criminal than the city punks. We had crimes of passion and violence; they were done in a violent moment and then either regretted or held as something to stay with to the death. We had bootleggers. We had men who had thieved, often because they were hungry or otherwise desperate. The sheriff often found jobs for these after they had served their term.

None of these men wanted a boy to follow his example.

Mr. Vinyard never asked anybody to follow his example either, but if you were a boy, he was the kind of person you hoped you would become.

There was a time in my life when I was all torn up trying to decide whether to be a taxidermist or a fingerprint expert. It started on a day when I was answering all the ads in *Popular Mechanics*.

At the time this was a monthly chore. I was still in the eleven-year-old bracket, but I had already discovered that one way to break the daily boredom of a small town was to write in for information from magazines. Back would come enough fascinating reading matter each morning to last the day, prospectuses on itch powder, esoteric treatises on machines to turn weaklings into muscle men, and plans for miniature prairie schooners.

The daily take had already grown beyond the capacity of the family lock box. Each day I showed up at the post-office window to take charge of a bushel basket of loot, and once the postmaster, Old Man Wulfman, a rather tired soul, asked whether I wasn't thinking about ordering a kitchen stove in the mail.

At the time, you could train for any career by correspondence. I remember a full-page ad in the old *Scribner's* magazine showing a woman who was remarking to her husband about the commanding figure that another man made at a party, and the husband was saying, "Yes, my dear, he knows The Law." Two careers caught my eye in this issue of *Popular Mechanics*. One ad said: "Earn Big Money! BE A TAXIDERMIST. Taxidermists earn up to $10 a day." The other read: "BE A DETECTIVE. Learn fingerprinting, the scientific method of crime detection. Excitement! Travel! Romance! Conversations with women!"

As you can see, the appeals in these ads are quite different, and a man had to give long thought to the conflict. The detective ad made no promise whatsoever of approaching ten dollars a day in income, and the taxidermy ad spoke nothing of conversations with women.

I sent for material on both jobs. In due time, I got an inch-thick portfolio from taxidermy showing pictures of fierce animals which had been stuffed and including letters from people who said they had never stuffed a kangaroo in their lives and then they took this course and stuffed a kangaroo. The fingerprinting kit included the secret reports of a detective. They clearly showed that he had traveled all the way from Philadelphia to Pittsburgh, but he seemed to be handicapped by having always to carry in his pocket a glass which he would hand people to get their fingerprints.

Then began a three-weeks wrestle with conscience and mind over the career to choose. It was aided by mailings from the two schools. After the third follow-up mailing, the taxidermy institute bluntly wanted to know whether I was chump enough to pass up the field and stated that it would mail no more. For six months, I got printed letters from fingerprints implying that open detective jobs were being filled fast. I might have taken the course if any money had been left after paying the stamp bill for answering the ads in a new month's issue of the magazine.

Of such slender things is a career in journalism made.

I first met Otis at a time when I was practicing being the Boy Reporter of the weekly newspaper.

Otis was a middle-aged man with a blue stubble and a black pompadour who habitually chewed a toothpick and looked shrewd. He was the town mayor. He was also the town barber, and a reporter could have an interview with Otis if he was willing to buy a haircut while he talked. Matter of fact, for the same service and fee, anybody could sit in on the town council session while Otis conducted the meeting.

His strong suit was economy in government.

"Otis," one of the aldermen would say, hitching a leg up over his arm of the barbershop waiting bench, "how about us putting a fireplug over there by the freight depot?"

Any such mention of city work always brought an emphatic shake of Otis' head.

"Hit'll cost money," he would object.

His proudest boast after each term of office was that the city had begun that term with $364 and ended it with $364.

There was a story behind that $364, too. The town government had solved the problem of tax income once simply by assessing each business house a fee for a permit to do business within the town. It was as good a way as any to raise money for the fire hose and cart.

It was also acceptable to the business people—except one. Old Lady Fry who ran a milliner's shop in the front room of her residence listened while the tax was explained. She then said she would be whipped before she would pay it and went on doing business.

When this was reported to Otis, he pointed out that she, of course, was laying herself open to the full penalties of the law. The fact was that the law hadn't provided any penalties, and nobody was going to risk the unpopularity that would come from voting a penalty. After that first assessment, the other business houses also neglected to pay their yearly tax, leaving the town government stranded with $364.

It was not wise to mention all this to Otis while getting a haircut. The hand with the scissors would begin to shake. He would get agitated and as venomous as anybody could get who was essentially kindhearted and friendly.

"All of 'em," he would almost hiss, "breakin' the law."

It was Otis who first revealed to me the fearfulness that hides in the hearts of those who cherish public office.

When time came to run for re-election, the Boy Reporter of the weekly paper did not have to buy a haircut to get an interview. Otis would seek him out at least twice a day.

"Have you heard of anybody gonna run yet?" Otis would ask anxiously.

Nobody ever ran against him, but by the filing deadline, Otis would be reduced to a jelly of a man.

When I left the place, he was still mayor. It is a good bet that he still is, if he is alive, and that the town still has that $364.

Constable Bunk Crow fancied his role as protector of life, limb, and temperance of Lariat townsfolk. So when he ran for sheriff against an incumbent whom we will simply call George, he took a militant stand on the traffic issue.

Bunk charged that some people had been helling around in autos at twenty miles an hour in the town limits.

"An octopus of crime has dug its feelers down amongst the entire 3241 people of the county," declared Bunk, "and George has fiddled when he should have been arresting."

As a matter of cold fact, George had been playing the guitar.

At the same time Bunk let everybody know that he was

going to enforce the law strictly, he reminded the voters that at least a dozen times within eight years George had needlessly harried and hectored a local citizen, even going so far as to arrest a few. This, said Bunk, was going to stop.

Asked how he was going to enforce the law more severely but cut down on arrests, Bunk replied, "I'm going to enforce it against them fellows from Amarillo and Clovis."

As I look back, it seems that about the only time a traffic law was enforced was against Sam.

Sam was a jittery local young man of twenty-plus years. He was wildly ambitious to become a successful bootlegger.

At regular intervals, he would go over to Clovis and pick up a suitcase full of pints for sale. Invariably, he would drink part of it before getting back to town and would end up by driving his Model T round and round the monument.

The monument was a simple shaft of Portland cement set in the middle of the highway, which was also the town's main street. On it was painted *California Trail* and the distances to all the cities in all directions. When making a U-turn at the corner, you were supposed to go around the monument. Few people bothered, however, because the monument was at the edge of town even if it was on the main business corner.

When a man like Sam began driving round and round the monument singing lustily, it was hard not to notice him.

Next morning Sam was always contrite about breaking the traffic laws, and he would agree to pay his fine in a few days. More often than not the suitcase of pints would disappear, but that was all right. After all, it wasn't fair to put Sam in double jeopardy.

Bunk, by the way, did not win the election.

Nevertheless, it was evident immediately that George had become a lot rougher on those fellows from Amarillo and Clovis.

To the elders of Lariat the "safe" job was earth's nearest point to heaven. Most of them had fought life catch-as-catch-can and had never had it safe. Their stock piece of advice was "Get yourself an education and a steady job." By a good job or steady job they meant a safe job indoors, like being stenographer to the county judge.

This advice never appealed much to the twelve-year-old rakehells of my generation. We had seen too many hints that, if one could escape that dry prairie town into the great world, all kinds of elegant mischief awaited the enterprising man. There was a great lady, a famous beauty, who had grown up in our town and used to come back from the city for an occasional visit. As messenger boy at Mr. Vinyard's passenger station, I used to help her get her luggage aboard the Chicago Missionary when she departed—in a Pullman car, no less. The whistle of the train on the horizon as it bore her away in the late afternoon was a trumpet telling of a world of fashion and fine wines, of people who wrote books and lived in abodes as magnificent as the gilt lobby of the Majestic Theater in Clovis.

Among the disturbers of the "safe" advice, Mr. O'Bannion was the greatest—if that was his name. It was the name he gave the sheriff. One night some Amarillo toughs tried to rob the town post office. There was a gun battle. When it ended, without wounds on either side, the towering figure of Mr. O'Bannion was discovered with a warm hogleg still in his hands. He courteously explained the mistake.

"I am but a poor wayfarer, friendless and far from home," he told the constable, wiping a tear from one china-blue eye. "Apparently I fell in among blackguards."

He was a six-foot-six man of great weight, potty, shambling, in the most monumental cowboy boots that a man ever wore. He was thrown into jail. There, through his barred first-floor window, he immediately made friends with the town boys. Mr. O'Bannion knew everything worth knowing. He knew how to make a heliograph. He knew how to cross-wire the bell in the basement of the church so that Sunday School could be disrupted thirty minutes early. His only fee for all this education was the price of an occasional sack of Bull Durham.

We learned of his past from yarns he told. He had fought and been court-martialed in the Boer War. He had been a filibusterer in Panama. He had been given the personal escort of a troop of cavalry out of Mexico for some mining operations he had been promoting. He was full of sage advice and ordinarily cheerful.

"Beware of false advisers, my son," he would say. "The devil guides their tongue to betray you to the pit."

It is true that once, when he thought he was alone, he

was heard to curse bitterly and to say that he had carried off better jails on his shoulders.

By the time of his trial, Mr. O'Bannion was a *cause célèbre* in our set, but he needn't have been. His defense was that he had just happened on the scene when the robbers were trying to break in. He conducted his own trial and managed somehow to imply a great contempt for the young prosecutor and a kinship between himself and the judge. For instance, he involved the court in a three-hour wrangle over whether he had killed two men in Panama. At the end he said to the prosecutor, "You young idiot, you haven't even qualified me as a witness."

A search of the record revealed that the prosecutor had indeed left out a question or something needed to qualify Mr. O'Bannion.

The prosecutor never was much good after that.

Mr. O'Bannion got off scot-free and left the courthouse amid a cloud of small boys. He was chewing on a nickel cigar he had cadged from the prosecutor.

"Never fear. Right will triumph," he told us. "Though in durance vile, be of good cheer. I will not forget you. I will always remember that you were friends in need. I must go now and arrange my train reservations. I have friends in Persia."

He departed shortly after on the rods of one of the refrigerator cars in the redball freight that slowed down on the rise east of town.

Mr. Cephius Cole was a large, fat, and expensive-looking man who used to run the Great Plains Trading Post.

The Great Plains was one of those L-shaped stores open-ing on two sides of a block that sold everything from shoe laces to steam tractors. It had a slogan on its small, be-grimed front window: *Credit Extended to All.*

Mr. Cole carried all the farmers in the territory from one harvest to the next and sometimes through two or three bad years. It was his theory that he couldn't ever afford to have all his customers pay their debts because he then would have no grounds for not paying his debts to the wholesalers, with whom he always stood high because of his business volume.

The prices he charged were outrageous. He would charge as much as twenty-nine cents a pound for the more expensive brands of coffee, but people preferred to trade with him rather than the people down the street who sold for much less but demanded cash. People looked on these characters as a chinchy lot who were probably out to gouge a customer of his last gold filling. Mr. Cole, in con-trast, was obviously a generous, open-handed man be-cause credit was extended to all.

Each year Mr. Cole collected what he could on account and sent what he could on account to the Chicago whole-salers, and everybody was happy.

Along in the Thirties, times got awfully tight and he went bankrupt, but he wasn't mad about it. After all, he said, they had been prosperous years while they lasted, and people had got a great deal of good out of the mer-chandise he had sold on credit. Also, thousands of shoe-makers, iron puddlers, coffee packagers, and other artisans back East had been kept employed by the goods the Great

Plains sold on credit. Mr. Cole always felt that the closing of his store might have caused the Great Depression. They happened about the same time.

Mr. Cole did not know that this country has always thrived on debt. Nobody ever talked about the millions in English investment money that went into developing West Texas. I don't know why. The statute of limitations has run out, and they can't get the money back.

Badger Pierce, a neighbor of ours, had a theory that the physical world was shrinking.

He said he had noticed it during his own lifetime. A stock tank where he had gone swimming as a boy was now not nearly as large as it had been then. He had also made careful observations at his eastern line fence, squinting up along a fencepost at the sun at exactly high noon, and it seemed to him that the fence had moved over a few feet to the west, doubtless because of the shrinkage.

Badger was dead set against the oil wells they were beginning to drill on the plains. It was obvious to him that, if they keep on pumping the insides out of the earth, the whole confounded thing would collapse under the weight of the locomotives, steam tractors, and other heavy objects roaming around on the crust.

I don't know where Badger latched onto his idea that the earth is growing smaller, but he soon became the county-wide expert on it.

He did a lot of reading to find out why the earth was shrinking, but never got much satisfaction. He was also a guileful pumper of information from the various physics teachers who came to our high school. Let a new science teacher show up, and Badger would find a way to corner him with the big question.

What explanation, Badger would demand, did science have for the shrinking of the earth?

The few who told him that they knew of no scientific evidence of the shrinking of the earth only angered Badger. He already knew it was shrinking. He wanted to know why. Most of the young science teachers, though, never gave him this much of an argument. I have an idea that each was suddenly confronted by the discovery that he didn't know whether the earth was shrinking or not.

Badger had rigged up his own machinery for measuring this shrinkage. He sank two steel pipes in concrete in the ground. They were exactly the length of a meter stick apart. Some of the high school boys had swiped the meter stick for Badger from the laboratory, and he admired it very much. It was science absolute.

With the meter stick, he would check the pipes from time to time waiting for the inevitable day when the shrinkage would draw them closer together.

Most people used to laugh at Badger.

Since I have grown older, though, I also have noticed that the world is shrinking.

In Lariat we were introduced to rock-and-roll music thirty years ahead of the rest of the country. Rock-and-roll is plain old West Texas honkytonk music. It has been taken out of the poolrooms and the shabby Saturday-night dance halls, but it is the same music, with the same squirmy rhythm, the same baying-at-the-moon style of singing. Every Lariat boy of twelve or older owned a guitar and aspired to this sort of music in the same way that he wore his hair long and soggy with brilliantine and had colored inserts put into the cuff seams of his blue jeans so they would have flashy bell bottoms.

Of course, none of us did any formal study of the guitar. Learning to read music was generally looked upon as unfairly cutting the corners. Obviously, if a man had really learned a piece on the guitar, he didn't need to write down notes to jog his memory about it.

The old-timers of our day objected to our style of using the guitar. They said it was not music. They argued that the guitar should be picked, an error into which such people as Segovia have fallen. It should play a melody. The West Texas style of playing was called chording. The guitar was used for percussion effects and for syncopation as it is in rock-and-roll.

On the whole, we of the plains sang about the usual rock-and-roll subjects. There were a lot of songs about the young woman who was so foolish as to leave the faithful singer for a man temporarily cutting a wider and gaudier swath. Unrequited love was popular, mainly because in our day all love at age fourteen was unrequited—you didn't have nerve enough to mention it to the girl.

Of course, my own interest in the guitar was more cultural. I learned the guitar to be able to sing Mexican folk songs. Particularly I wanted to sing "La Paloma," which isn't much of a folk song, but I thought it was. It was some time after learning the guitar that I noticed that I had forgotten to learn Spanish, and gradually the guitar was moved out to the storeroom along with the old horned-frog husks.

I have it from Howard Hill, an old bandsman who is mostly known around Dallas as Rats, that this is just as well. He says there is no way to quit playing "La Paloma." He says that the ending runs back into the beginning, so that the music goes round and round without ever coming out anywhere except back where you started.

There is no place for a finishing crescendo, no way to put a period to the music, he says, so that you go on playing the same thing for several hours and then say "That's all, folks."

It is a horrible thing, says Mr. Hill, to run into a song that defeats the human will to quit.

I learned to play golf before they put all that silly grass on the greens to throw your putts off.

The links where I learned golf years ago in West Texas had good sand greens. You could tell the greens from the fairways because the greens were oiled. Off to one side of the playing area they had a few grass hazards, but the main hazard on this course was called J. C. Temple's bull. This was on Number 3, a long dogleg so placed that the lower half of the leg ran alongside the *XIT* pasture, where the first drive was almost certain to land.

Properly speaking, it wasn't Mr. Temple's bull, but he ran the pasture where the bull was kept, and the bull regarded all golf clubs *ipso facto* weapons of aggression.

It was one of the worst hazards to concentrate in you can imagine.

This was a good course, though, and produced plenty of minor-league .300 hitters and punters who could kick sixty yards as well as some people who can knock a golf ball pretty good through grass.

The course had other hazards besides J. C. Temple's bull. On Number 7, under a beargrass just into the rough, was a ground rattler who sometimes showed and sometimes didn't. Mostly he didn't but he sure kept you guessing.

On one of the other fairways was a tiny prairie-dog town, and if you landed there, you had reached the point of no return to the links. Most people don't think of grass as a trap, but they have never tried to play a ball after it has landed in a tight-fitting pocket formed by four clumps of buffalo grass.

The main hazard I faced, however, was my own game. I never could drive as far with a driver as with a mashie; on the other hand, a wooden driver was a far better precision club than an iron. The game was further complicated by my ability to shoot a birdie on one hole and never come close to the pin on another. When this happened, the other players usually conceded any putt within throwing distance of the green to keep the game moving. I have made a hole in one, and some holes I have never made.

The memory of why I gave up golf is not clear. For some time I had been awakening in the middle of the night in high anger at some defect in my driver or mashie. The

last ball I ever hit was a drive. Everybody stood back—
as they usually did when I had a club in my hand—and I
hit the usual screamer. This time the ball didn't do its
usual violent curve to left or right. It went straight. That
was a long hole, but the ball overshot the green. It overshot the course. It overshot the three-strand barbed-wire
fence beyond the links.

When I reached the green, the ball was two hundred
yards beyond it and on the way home. I looked at it and
over at J. C. Temple's bull. "Why not?" I said, and went
home. I would still like to know: Why not?

The goathead burr is part of West Texas civilization.
It is a hard, nutlike burr shaped like a goat's head, which
manages to keep two of its needlelike thorns always upward in position to ram.

It is largely responsible for the vigor and pungency of
ten-year-olds' prairie speech.

It is hard to do justice exactly to the goathead burr,
though it is generally easy to find one. Take a look at some
youngster as he is racing barefoot across the prairie. Suddenly, he will rise ten feet in the air and run six or seven
superhuman strides while suspended.

This is the tipoff that he has hit a patch of goathead
burrs, also called heel burrs or the devil's head. It was also
once mistakenly called the grass burr, possibly because it
was the nearest thing to grass that would grow on the soil
where it was generally found.

You no doubt remember Aesop's story about how Andro-
cles made a lifetime friend of a lion by pulling a thorn

from the animal's paw. Aesop has got one detail wrong here. Quite obviously it was a goathead burr and not a thorn that was bothering the lion. I have known really fierce animals like the ground squirrel or the West Texas mouse to lose their wildness and beseech human aid when afflicted with a goathead burr. This burr not only hurts when it hits. It later produces a kind of cold shivering like the sting of a red ant.

Also, the spike, when broken off, seems to travel on through whatever substance it hits. At Lariat, an old stove-up cowpuncher known to everybody as Uriah got one in his left forefoot. He had sprained his ankle so that he couldn't get that foot in his boot, and he was hobbling around barefoot.

It made the usual festering sore and disappeared. Eleven years later, a festering appeared on the lobe of his left ear and the spike of the burr emerged. As he said, it narrowly missed the brain. It is a tribute to the goathead burr that Uncle Uriah had no trouble remembering when he first got it.

A little Korean girl exchange student was attending Wayland College out in Plainview. Somebody asked her how she liked the plains country.

"Well," she said, "there just isn't anything to lean your eyes against, is there?"

This is a misconception common to newcomers on the high baldies.

It was one of the things that dismayed newcomers from the timbered countries. No place to lean—not post or tree or rock. In those days, one of my uncles a couple of times removed almost broke his neck trying to lean on a mirage.

He was a woods countryman and had trouble with mirages all his life. Once he tried to run through a three-strand barbed-wire fence, thinking it was a mirage.

Eventually people accustomed themselves to their new geography and found that the plains had one of the best of all things to lean on—the wind. At Bovina I once saw a couple of men chat for a quarter of an hour while leaning comfortably on the air at a forty-five-degree angle.

This was in a little April zephyr impressive only to people in parts of the country where a wind is thought to be a wind merely because it blows over one or two un-calibrated old ladies or uproots a few trees. In the Lariat country, when the loose two-by-fours on the barn start standing out in the breeze you have a mildly strong wind. When the spikes start working loose on the windmill tower, it is really making up to blow.

In the worst of our dust storms, when whole counties took wing, we never lost any trees. In the first place, there weren't any to speak of. In the next place, the few trees that did grow were proper trees for the dust-storm country. They were locusts.

The locust is a mildly paranoid tree. It grows from a sapling with the conviction that every man's hand is against it. Thorns on the trunk and branches discourage climbers. There are few limbs for a bird to hang a nest on, and the locust never puts out enough leaves to encourage anyone to stand in its shade. Although the locust is runty and not much taller than a tall man, it has a taproot that goes deep into the earth, wraps its finger around solid granite, and holds on.

The roots from this tree send up little shoots all over the countryside which are hard to dig out, and the root system goes all over the earth. I knew a farmer who had one at his kitchen door where it could catch the dishwater. One day his neighbor came over from beyond the line fence a quarter of a mile away and told the man to get his confounded locust out of his field.

The locust fits the country just as man learned to do.

As man grew used to the flat tableland, he found that the wind was one of the best tools he had.

It pumped virtually all the water on the high plains in the early years. It turned electric generators. It provided gently sloping sand ramps along the fences so that one could just walk over them. And it was one of the best garbage-disposal systems ever to turn up. Many an early settler of the Panhandle region can remember passing a small West Texas town in the late afternoon and seeing the whole day's accumulation of trash departing on a whirl-wind.

On recent trips to the plains I have noticed with sad-ness that the windmill is losing out on farms to gasoline-driven water pumps. The windmill was one of the few poetic signs in that stark country, and many a prairie Wordsworth has begun a poem with "My heart leaps up when I behold windmills against the sky."

However, the windmill water pump didn't cost much and, like everything that doesn't cost much, a man can't afford it. It puts him in a higher income-tax bracket.

Soon the windmill will be only a remembered music of

groan, clash, and clatter, atonality at its best; but even though it is going the way of the horse, it left its imprint on the plains country in a form of a business firm that exists nowhere else, so far as I know. This business was called the windmill supply house.

A windmill supply house naturally does not sell windmills or windmill parts—not any more. It sells Savage arms, shower-curtain rods, Tinker Toys, electric washing machines, TV sets, and pickup truck covers. Nevertheless it once dealt in windmills, and the name survives; and there is a big windmill supply house in Lubbock that still keeps a couple of windmills in stock. Some of these business houses have sentiment.

The *Morning News'* book editor, Lon Tinkle, is a gourmet of both capacity and discrimination. He came back once from a meeting of the Confrerie des Chevaliers du Tastevin in Dallas with the idea that something ought to be done for the gourmet's world at Lariat.

He thought I might be able to come up with some creations involving the hot dog or chili, but the wiener out on the high baldies was looked on as one of those fancy, frivolous foreign foods, fine for savor and bouquet but nothing to stick to a man's ribs. In our country, people ate beef. It wasn't steak, exactly, or roast. More often it was fried cow, sometimes served with flour gravy.

The West Texas food lover came from an individualistic tradition. The gourmets in Dallas and other big towns like to give a dish a descriptive name to make it sound more attractive. On the menu, for instance, you will find such things as "Caviar de Beluga." Out West we also gave food descriptive names, but they weren't supposed to make the food sound more attractive. They strove for accuracy. Certainly, no true West Texas gentleman would have put these terms in print.

The expert on fine food in our whole end of the world was a cowboy named Bill Perry, who used to ride the caboose to Kansas City all the time with the cattle cars.

Anybody who shipped cattle was entitled to send one man free in the caboose to help feed and water the stock on the way. Bill, being a bachelor, usually took on this trip. That is how he became West Texas' best-traveled man between Hereford and Kansas City and also a food expert. He had tried all the fancy places, the Stockyards Cafe, the Breeders and Brand Inspector's Bar, the Stockman's Tavern. He found them inferior to the fare cooked up on the caboose stove, especially if somebody had accidentally dropped a crate of oranges while moving them in a refrigerator car, or the train had passed close by a fat chicken and damaged its heart, as often happened, so that it had to be put out of its misery.

Bill disapproved of those fancy Kansas City places. He said they were given to silly waste.

"In one place where I was at," he said, with a disapproving scowl, "everybody had two forks."

The West Texas gourmet would never have gone along with the serving of fine wines at a dinner. He might cultivate his appetite with a pint of whiskey behind the barn, but wine was patently a sinful drink. The churches all used Concord grape juice in communions.

The West Texan was not likely to fly in a chef all the way from New York to prepare a meal, either. A ranchowner who was going to send out a chuckwagon would look carefully into the qualifications of the local cooks available.

"Who is laid up?" he would demand of the hands. The superb qualification for cooking was a cast on an ankle or a burden of years too heavy to allow a man to get on a horse.

It was not considered good practice to make the chuckwagon food too good. It might keep the men from their work and also might increase the cost by five or ten dollars. A man was supposed to do his work on the round-up and do his big eating on his own time.

The surest sign that the wheel of the year had come full turn in Lariat was the appearance of the St. Joseph's aspirin calendar, a piece of popular literature of the order of the Sears catalog.

This calendar is one of those old-time wall jobs that tell everything a year in advance. Look ahead a year to a January day, for instance, and you find the following: "Blustery. Sun rises at 7:03, sets 5:00. Moon sets 7:05. Epiphany. Fishing fair in the evening. Sun in the sign of Capricorn." And further notes that, despite storminess elsewhere, the day will be pleasant in California and a warning, astrologically speaking, that it isn't a good day to plant anything.

In Lariat, a St. Joseph's calendar on the kitchen wall was the mark of a family that kept itself informed. The man who didn't keep one was always having to kite around over the countryside trying to find someone who knew when the next dark of the moon was going to show. Everybody knows you can't plant turnips in the dark of the moon.

The St. Joseph's calendar was the mark of an informed family but one of the common, plebeian variety. Cultured families bought a "religious thoughts" calendar. In addition to all the information about the weather and the dark of the moon, this calendar had a daily Scripture quotation, something like "Suffer little children to come unto Me." Each page was decorated with a colored Sunday-school picture and was bordered in heavy gilt.

Of course, the families who bought this calendar had other signs by which you knew they were cultured. There were the books on the living-room standtable, a tall square table with each leg ending in a bronze claw that grasped a glass ball. The books were always the Holy Bible and that *Rubaiyat of Omar Khayyam*. No one apparently saw anything inconsistent in combining Holy Writ with that exhortation to drink, for you know not why you go nor where. And indeed, there isn't any inconsistency if you just look at the covers of the books. Later on, H. G. Wells' *Outline of History* made its appearance on the table, after it had come down to ninety-eight cents in the cloth binding, and it lay there with the other two books, despite its essay on evolution—a comfortable assurance that the family had it all, all of history, trapped there in the front room.

The calendars, however, were useful culture.

Don't think an aspirin company was trying to cut its

own throat in predicting the weather right on the nose for a year in Texas. Outsmarting the weather is the biggest cause of headaches down here.

Nevertheless, the St. Joseph's calendar tried it. A lot of people doubt that it can say dogmatically that September 3, nine months away, will be stormy. One summer I checked all the predictions for June against the weather that actually developed. Nearly every day, for at least a minute or so, I noticed weather something like that predicted by the calendar. Some days I had to strain hard, but I did it.

Jesse Guy Smith at Commerce has raised an objection to my kind of Lariat.

"My daily perusal and enjoyment of Big D has got me interested in Lariat, Texas," he wrote. "For a time I was not sure that there was a place by that name but only a fictitious town of yours. The more I read the more interested I became in this queer, unusual town.

"I visited it last week. Your slant is far from the present-day Lariat. It is beautiful country. That irrigation giving it the verdant hue may be later than your boyhood views, but it is wonderful now. . . . I like Lariat."

It is true that Lariat is about to progress me out of anything to write about. Time is about to euchre me out of it.

Lariat has matured now. It has a population of two hundred. It has a tree, which gives it a gardened look. They have found a new diamond-tipped bit or something that will dig wells on the high plains, and the fields are all rich and well watered. At the beginning, we often didn't have much water. We used to have to shoo the cattle out of sight of the draws when the rains filled them. The sight of any body of water larger than a twenty-foot earth tank six inches deep made the cattle lose weight. They apparently got seasick.

Of course, things weren't really as bad as that. We may have been poor, often thirsty, and sometimes hungry, but all of us on the plains in those days were handsome.

It seems in memory wonderful country. The Lariat that I remember was that village of three or four buildings, a lot of dryland farms, and enough unbroken grassland to run a horse in.

The country I remember was the boundless acres of tableland between the Rockies and the caprock, a plain in which a distant house was a dot and a man a speck, and the tides of white moonlight that flooded it at night, moonlight and the yucca flowers that stretched dimly white toward the horizon, and great grass carpet waving in the cool wind, moonlight and the smudgy wall of night beyond which lurked the shades of the Spanish wanderers and the Comanches and the dreams that ached in a young animal's heart but were not clear in his mind.

I admit to the richness and the softness and the luxuriance of the Panhandle landscape generally now, but not to a beauty superior to that I knew. For the landscape that moves a man most powerfully is the landscape in his mind, the country that comes back in dreams and unguarded reveries. It grew up in his mind when he wasn't looking.

4

A RIGHT SMART
WINDMILL FIXER

A long time ago some of us began to make occasional intensive five-minute efforts to get down on paper the language people really use instead of the language the dictionaries say they use. It is a crushing burden because it involves, of course, translating the English language.

The country has me to thank for finding out what *stovepiping the beans* meant before the Russians knew. It all started back when Gayle Smith, Sr., a student of artistic Texas expression, came up with some material for the Texas Common Reader. How about, he asked, the phrase *windmill fixer*, meaning a know-it-all, and the old expression, *He stovepiped the beans*, meaning that the man lied?

You could tell at a glance that Mr. Smith was right about windmill fixer, which properly means a man who talks a good job at doing anything, one with a spiel, one whose merchandise is words. Nobody knows when it first appeared, but it came out of an old description of a studhorse sort of man which listed his attributes, concluding:

"... and a fighter, and a wildhorse rider, and a right smart windmill fixer."

As for stovepiping the beans, that was something else. It was suspect from the beginning and seemed more Alaskan than Texan. After all, the dried bean is known as the national citrus fruit in Alaska. Texans, unassuming people, have never cared much for beans or milk or steak. They liked fried beef.

Frank Conrad of Dallas furnished the answer. He says it came from a practice of sacking beans to hide the bad ones. In stovepiping beans, you put a layer of choice beans in the bottom of a hundred-pound sack. Then you put in a section of stovepipe and pour good beans around it. You pour the cull beans and trash and maybe some rocks or dirt inside the stovepipe, pull it out, and top the sack with some more of the high-quality beans.

You might think from this that *stovepiping the beans* came from East Texas, the black-eyed pea capital of the world, but Melvin Mailloux, a Yankee come to Dallas, said that he used to do the same thing with onions when he worked on Connecticut Valley farms during his school-days. By using the stovepipe, a layer of fine onions could be sacked around a core of rotten ones.

Mailloux once asked an old Polish-American farmer who first thought of the idea.

"Everybody did it in Poland," said the old man.

The tracing of quaint folk ways of speaking to the source takes a lifetime of painstaking scholarship. My most recent spare-time contribution to the lore came about when a lady with a sensitive ear took exception to the Texas practice of saying *whelp* for *welt*.

People say it here, it's true. I know a Phi Beta Kappa girl out of one of the state's better universities who talks about whelps whenever one appears.

It is unfair to charge Texas with this particular whelp on the purity of English, however. The usage was first noticed almost fifty years ago in western Indiana. Within ten years, people were bothered by whelps in places as far apart as Richmond and New Orleans. In New Orleans, *whelp* was a word of the Anglos rather than the whites of French descent, which lends some support to the idea that it was brought in from England. This suspicion is strengthened by the ancient inability of the English tongue to handle *h*. It takes no great memory to recall such variants as the Cockney *h*, the kind of *h* that crops out in *gunnels* and the *h* that was used by an old-timer I once knew who talked about a horse's *whithers*. A variant of whelp in the form of *whelt* has existed a long time in the mountain regions of Kentucky, Tennessee, and North Carolina, and in the Ozarks.

The evidence seems to suggest that *whelp* came out of the mountain regions of the East, as have so many fine old American expressions and worthless pieces of antique furniture. Like *antigodlin* and *whaunkerjawed,* whelp originated on the eastern seaboard and moved west. The pull of the moon probably has something to do with it. This may be the reason that California has never contributed much in the way of picturesque speech.

According to my calculations, language in the form of

folk nouns and folk adjectives seems generally to move from east to west until it covers the country and becomes part of general usage. The verb phrase *to light a shuck*, for instance, certainly originated in the eastern mountains but is now common language in El Paso. *To poormouth* is also now in national usage, though possibly it is not used much in Texas, where people do not have the habit of minimizing their assets.

From now on, when anybody invents one of these picturesque American phrases, I wish he would make a record of the time and place. Just take out an old envelope right then. Jot on it: "On Jan. 31, 1961, I said——"

It would save a lot of work. This is the conclusion one reaches after trying several days to find the origin of the saying *He laid out with the dry cattle*. It was a common enough cow-country saying, expressing the sober citizen's disapproval of a real heller, a wastrel. After a week of digging in learned volumes, you'll decide that the saying never existed.

One old-time westerner did take the trouble to jot down a couple of words once, and he furnished the history for the verb *buffalo* and the noun *stinker*. The first man to buffalo another was a frontier marshal. In those days buffaloing a man meant disarming him by laying the barrel of a Colt alongside his head. One of the greatest sutlers to the buffalo-hunting trade has so testified, just as he also recorded that a stinker, like your neighbor's son, was originally a low-lifer who went around in the spring thaw skinning buffalo self-respecting hunters had killed the fall before. The animals had been frozen before they could be skinned, and when they had thawed out enough for the skinning knife to bite in, they smelled up the prairie. No doubt about it, that fellow had done firsthand research and was an authentic folklorist. You could take his word for it.

Back when Ralph Yarborough was still running against Allan Shivers for Governor, a certain Dallas man fled one day to an East Texas fishing lake seeking some spot where he could get away from all the political yak.

He had a fine, peaceful day, but that night he couldn't sleep for the sound of the frogs. At first he didn't understand it. Then he realized that he was hearing a big bull-frog boom "Yarbor, Yarbor, Yarbor" all through the night. And a frog chorus would answer, "Shivers, Shivers, Shivers." The Dallas man returned home rather shaken.

Actually, this man was lucky, and most of us would have given a pretty to have had his experience. Obviously, he was hearing from the forks of the creek, and he is the only man on record who ever did.

Generations of Texas politicians, trailing by a few votes, have said "Wait till you hear from the forks of the creek." I have listened with some of them for the sound of a big frog up there trumpeting their name or at least a chorus of little voices. I have not yet heard from the forks of the creek.

It is my theory that you can hear what they say up there, but you can't tell which way they will jump.

The fount of Texas English undefiled is threatened these days by people moving in from regions where they call a plain old "ro-de-yo" a "ro-DAY-o." It is enough to make Texans start writing letters to the London *Times*.

These misguided people do worse than introduce a barbaric pronunciation. They question even the purest of our usages. Just after one of our staff men had turned in his weekly Central Texas epic recently he was attacked by a lady from east of the Sabine. She objected to the use of *stove-up*. You do not find stove-up, she said, in the dictionary.

You do not find your cufflinks in the dictionary, either. Stove-up people know what they are before they look in the dictionary. The best way to find out the meaning of stove-up is to ride a horse.

You will find stove-up in the *American Thesaurus of Slang,* where it doesn't belong. This thesaurus equates stove-up with such classical English expressions as *done up, jiggered up, corked out,* and *pooped.* The Texas kind of stove-up has nothing to do with these. Corked out, for instance, is a nautical expression. Any old sailor can tell you that it came from putting corking in the seams of a wooden ship.

In a man who is stove-up, the ball ends of his knee-bones and elbows have busted backward through the sockets so that he does not really walk. He crips around. He has no teeth, so the surface of his chin is clamped firmly against the end of his nose. Since his eyes have gone bad, he squints one and flutters the other when he works up a glare. A man like this is eminently qualified as a fine range cook even if he has never touched a frying pan.

Another northerner who has recently pitched camp in Dallas raised the dickens about our expression *plum nelly.*

This is a pure, antique expression that is heard too little recently. The proper form of it is *plum and nelly.* It is properly used as in the expression *plum out of Tenaha and nelly over to Timpson,* which accurately describes the spot you have reached.

" 'Plum nelly' is a bit redundant," says Jim Neal, an East Texas expert. "Plum . . . and nelly on the other hand has a nice easy cadence and is still in wide usage."

There is no excuse for ignorance about this term. There is a community named Plum Nelly back east somewhere in Tennessee.

It is important for the tenderfoot Texas talker not to confuse plum and nelly with *perten nelly,* which means almost.

Generally speaking, the eastern folk drift into error in Southwestern speech through trying to be logical. They give *rodeo* its full Spanish spin when they pronounce it because they imagine that it came from the *caballeros.* The rodeo came from the boredom of Texas cow-country Sunday afternoons. People who had ridden broncs and roped cattle all week for pay and keep gathered to amuse themselves by riding broncs and roping cattle. They called the get-together a ro-de-yo because they didn't know what the English word for it was. The rodeo is no more Mexican than chop suey is Chinese. It is no more Mexican than Texas chili, that high-flavored meat soup which developed in the greasy-spoon restaurants of Texas. Only in these cafés do you find the fine disregard for ingredients which makes genuine chili.

A man named Philip Rader came down to Dallas a few

years ago to teach football and history at one of the junior
high schools. When he got the answers to one of his first
examinations on medieval European history, he was fairly
astounded.

He learned that *serf* is a washing powder, *manor* is a
bakery and *monopoly* is a game.

All these are perfectly good colloquial meanings down
here in Texas, of course. How is a mere Minnesotan to
know that down here *vassal* is a stuff they make a salve
out of? Back in the Dark Ages, a knight may have been
held *in durance vile,* but down here that means the football team is in lousy shape.

Still, we wish Mr. Rader would extend the exam sometime. I'd like to know what *fief* and *feudal contract* mean
locally.

Some of us were wondering the other night what became of the old-time practice of *bending an effort.*

About the last time anybody heard of this practice was
in some manuals that the Navy whipped up during World
War II to train young, weak-minded reserves up to the
rigors of the service. "Bend every effort!" these manuals
would scream, with exclamation marks, in the same tone
used to exhort the young and flabby-willed to flemish or
fake down every line. For all I know, the Navy is still
bending efforts. Military services, they say, are traditional-
minded, and if it has been tradition to bend every effort,
they will continue to be bent even if other folks are beginning to use efforts straight.

Some reserves not too far from my desk ended the war

with a foggy notion that an effort was part of the ship's equipment.

Anyhow, any reasonably mature person can remember the time when no good business had any use for straight efforts. All had to be bent. High school graduates emerged from each commencement speech with biceps tensed to bend every effort they might encounter.

An employer of my acquaintance says that it isn't just the bent effort that is disappearing. Efforts themselves, he says, are on their way out.

The unfashionableness of the bent effort suggests that the world is changing. We see evidence of it in other ways. The long arm of coincidence, for instance, withered years ago to a mere stump and is rarely heard about now. Time was when it grabbed half the offenders arrested by the police department.

It is true that quite a few people still make no bones about things and that others are still barking up the wrong tree. There are still a few pretty kettles of fish around, although I have not personally seen one in quite a while. Welcome reliefs are still abundant, too. Almost nobody has a crow to pick any more, though. Picking crow with somebody has stopped being an acceptable way to kill time. It may be that fewer people eat crow.

Nobody has nailed a lie to the counter in years. Maybe they don't trust modern building materials.

And there are few towering ambitions. It used to be said of a friend of mine that he had a towering ambition to be precinct chairman at Lariat.

One of the losses to literature in this process was the villain who grinned like a Cheshire cat. A villain always used to grin like a Cheshire cat, and you could tell he was no good from that first grin.

Nowadays, villains do not grin like cats. They snap, rasp, grunt, or leer. If a villain these days ever grinned like a Cheshire cat, the hero would demand to know what gives with this guy? Is he nuts?

All this has got away, though, from bent efforts. We're saving a bunch of old, useless ones for antiques.

For some time it has been apparent that poetry in English is going to be put on a sounder basis by television. It will get to be more down-to-earth with less wild stuff about hark, the lark at heaven's gate doth sing, when actually the lark is singing in some Jimson weeds. At Garland, outside Dallas, Mrs. Charles Meyers was having her third-graders write some poems about the month of March, a subject to trick a poet into purple fustian if there ever was one. Her prize rhymester came up with:

> March is here.
> April's near.
> I think it's time for a glass of beer.

In this the discerning critic can see the influence of TV between-the-acts poetry. It presages a coming of what the future may call the Milwaukee School of American Poetry. This school will quickly correct the common misconception that Falstaff is a character in Shakespeare and will raise "Thinks't thou because thou art virtuous, Malvolio . . ." to the point of high esteem that it merits.

Poets always were better at writing about nightingales than hoot owls, though the hoot owl is a fact of life that has to be faced. The Milwaukee School may force them to hear the owl hoot. Before the Milwaukee School came along, English poetry had got itself into sad shape by singing of things as they ought to be rather than as they are. Take all those poems about how sweet the nightingale sings off in the night. Actually, the nightingale doesn't sing very good; his name just sounds as if he ought to. This sort of thing later led American poets into error when they tried to pick an American bird for their poems to fill the nightingale's place in English lines. First they tried to pick out one that could sing, and birds that can sing hardly ever rhyme very good. The whippoorwill, for instance, never caught on, though a lot of poets used him.

The Americans did a little better when they picked the mockingbird, but about all you can write about his song is "Listen to the mockingbird," because nobody knows what he is going to sing next.

Meanwhile, the facts of life remain undeniable. Anybody who has ever heard an owl at close quarters is not going to forget it soon. Owls have promoted more romance than all the nightingales and larks put together. You do not have to say "Ah, love, hark to the owl," because she has already harked and is ready for some close-quarters company.

There may have been some excuse for bird poets once,

but not now. In our modern and highly specialized age, a man has to make up his mind whether he wants to be a birdwatcher or a poet. He cannot appear as an expert in both on TV.

By the fresh standards of the Milwaukee School, some of the old-timers are not going to rank so high. None of them ever wrote much about cosmetics, for instance, except Alexander Pope, and he was pretty sneering. I do not see him appearing for Revlon. Also, no matter how beautifully Swinburne could write about real estate, it doesn't exactly fit the GI house.

The California wine industry might have used Fitzgerald if his approach had not been so gloomy and negative. He should have busied himself with producing immortal song on how much better the wine on your table ought to be than the sorry stuff served up by your neighbor.

Great-aunt Martha demanded stern things of people. She had no use for bird hunters and devotees of other such fleshly pleasures. She had no use for fiddlers for the sound reason, as she said, that Satan finds things. As a child, I often witnessed her disapproval of another kind of person who seemed harmless enough and might even be liked by other good church people. He might be a young man of whom most people spoke well, but Aunt Martha would shake her head over him.

"He reads novels," she would say darkly.

Her tone of voice implied one of those sins *in camera,* a private indulgence like taking morphine which was of no public moment but was folly, folly, folly and would lead to no good. After all these years and thousands of novels read, the word *novel* to me still has overtones of tragic self-indulgence and fatal flaws of character. It might speak of talent wasted, but Aunt Martha did not believe in talent. She believed only in work, though she might admit that a person had a turn for a certain kind of work.

When Aunt Martha visited a house where there was a book, she kept a wary distance from it until she could find out whether it was a sound volume. It was not reading she objected to. It was the novel. She said, heavens, it was all right to read some uplifting work if a body didn't have anything to do. The shall's and shall-not's of Leviticus were excellent reading. So was a good Baptist pamphlet entitled "Hell Through Error: An Examination of the Campbellites."

It was all right to read arithmetic or to study in the almanac the proper signs under which to perform the farm tasks, and Aunt Martha's catholicity extended even to the weekly Kansas City *Star*. When her husband got down his glasses and took up his spot in the rocker on the front porch with his paper in his hand, she would shoo all the kids away.

"Quiet!" she would order. "Papa is going to read."

And, assuming the correct reading posture in the rocker, the old man would read for a time, stopping frequently to deliver emphatic opinions on the IWW, the middlemen who were ruining the farmers, and the utterly whimsical variations of the price of steers on the Kansas City markets.

Aunt Martha thought nothing of it when the youngsters were learning to spell and do sums, but she was thunderstruck when she learned the schools were teaching them the "lies" of the Arthurian legends.

She believed firmly that a sentence existed to be parsed rather than read. Yet, when I think back on some of the novels that were popular in our country in those days, I think she may have been right about them.

One of them was an early-day soap opera called *Sunshine and Shadow*. Another was called *Surrey of Eagle's Nest*, if I remember right. *The Girl of the Limberlost* was everywhere that the *Trail of the Lonesome Pine* led. The high priest of the crowd was Harold Bell Wright, with his battles of virtue and vice and great whirlpools in which the evil was sucked down.

They were a violation of the magic of the novel. Aunt Martha was right in feeling that there wasn't really anything there except the illusion, nothing that a body could fix her mind to.

But then Aunt Martha disapproved of the magic itself.

A sad thing is happening to newspapering. The filler has all but disappeared. Those little paragraphs without headlines that used to fill out the column are all but gone. Maybe you had been reading a long story about Methodist ministers assigned here and there for the year. It was three lines short of filling the column, so you came on a jim dash and then the paragraph: "The monkeys have no tails in Zamboanga." That was a filler.

For a long time I have secretly believed that all people who have a liberal education got it from reading fillers. The filler compressed all knowledge a bit at a time into one sentence. A close reader of fillers is bound to range the field of human knowledge. One of the best ones ever printed, truly a classic, is this: "Ninety per cent of the ships entering the harbor of Mozambique are dhows." Think of it! Where besides a filler would you ever find this fascinating information?

And there was "In Afghanistan, 131,641 persons starved to death in the famine of 1825." So far as I know all the so-called historians have missed this fact entirely.

It was from a filler years ago that some of us learned that Shakespeare was a Mason. Other people have disputed this since, but I have never seen any filler retracting it.

The filler writers were among the first men to cultivate the advancement of science. A whole generation of men thus learned that "Male seahorses have pouches like kangaroos" and "The wry-billed plover of New Zealand is the only bird with a bill which is bent sideways."

Of course, the business of publishing fillers had its sloppy practitioners. One-line fillers, items of five words or less, are hard to come by and were often overdone.

I once worked for a country editor who made up his own pages and composed cooking recipes to fit the holes. As a buck linotype operator, I could set type just fast enough to take down the fillers as he dictated them. If the filler was a line short, the editor always said: "Then add another tablespoon of butter."

The greatest piece of compressed edification that has ever come to my attention was a one-line filler that read "Bees have no knees." This masterpiece was immediately recognized as such by all the printers, each of whom hastened to hide away a linotype slug bearing it. For several weeks the paper informed readers in two or three places every issue that bees have no knees.

The publisher finally tired of this scoop and wrote a note saying that bees no longer had no knees around our paper.

The press agents still grind out an assortment of fillers for small newspapers to use. However, the present crop, though piquant and terse, seems inferior in authoritativeness and exactness. Consider the old-timer: "Two thousand, five hundred and ninety-one of the inhabitants of Franz Josef Land have pellagra." There was authoritativeness. Compare this with "The great auk became extinct about 1844. Today there are not more than eighty mounted specimens in the world," a filler I recently clipped from a colleague's paper.

The joker here is that phrase "about 1844." Either the great auk became extinct in 1844, or he didn't. There is no "about" it. An old-fashioned filler would have pegged this down.

Another example of the slack kind of writing that goes into the modern filler is this one from the Associated Press: "The Federal Housing Administration reports that about thirty per cent of the houses sold annually in the U.S. are new homes. The rest are used homes."

The filler writer here has simply jumped to a conclusion. How does he know that "the rest are used homes?" He doesn't. He overlooks a kind of home that has become fairly common since the Federal Housing Administration got into the act. This is the purgatory home. This is a home which is bought new by a buyer who discovers something dreadfully wrong with the foundation before he moves in. He is trying to unload it.

About twenty per cent of the homes on sale at any given time are purgatory homes. The furnace doesn't work right or there is a live railroad track across the back yard or the buyer didn't want that kind of house after all.

On the whole, the FHA filler runs a little like an old-time one: "Almost all books have an equal number of even and odd pages."

Well-edited newspapers no longer like fillers much. They edit the story to fit the space and laugh at the filler as a harmless but naïve device. It wasn't always so harmless. A county-seat editor in a hardshell Texas town used to be given to printing "canned" fillers that were mailed in. Without knowing it, he printed one that read: "The first bourbon whiskey was distilled by a Baptist minister." Next day he didn't have a paper.

There are ways and ways of viewing history and the records that purport to bear tidings of man's past. The newspapers carried a story about how the Air Force had acted vigorously to preserve one of its "historic" sites where something happened in 1944. Everybody sniggered a little, conveniently forgetting that history for the Navy comes later than history as the Army sees it. As a matter of fact, history in the Navy's eyes didn't start until it was separated from the Army. And, if you get right down to it, military people aren't the only ones who find very little of historical worth that isn't connected with them.

There was the Greek historian who wrote that nothing worthwhile had happened before his lifetime, and I have personally noticed that the things that happened before I was born are not anything like as valuable as the things that have happened since. Marion the Swamp Fox was passably interesting, and that story about how Ben Franklin used to slip essays under the door of his brother's printing office is a good one. The old-timers were just not as important as we present-day people, though, and there will be very little left for the youngsters to do when our generation has wound up all its important projects.

Out in the neighborhood of Lariat, Texas, when I was a boy, the old-timer called Uncle Uriah by the community was a dried-up, knotty-foreheaded little man with a stubborn eye and crafty ways. If you told him the world was round, he was apt to peer at you suspiciously. Tell him that Eli Whitney invented the cotton gin, and he was pretty sure he was getting a con job.

"That so? Did you see it?" he would demand; or "If this is so, why ain't I heard about it?"

Uncle Uriah spoke for the human race.

Take yourself. Washington was a great man and Father of His Country, but do you really think he could handle your problems?

Americans may talk a lot about history, especially in political speeches, but watch them in argument. The American takes whatever bit from history serves his purpose and lets the rest go hang. The result is a view of history that likely as not proves exactly what he is saying.

A translator is one literary fellow who is generally ignored and never gets himself in the limelight although he lights up dark corners for others. Except for him we would not be able to understand many of the masterpieces of literature; even as it is, we are sometimes left wondering whether he actually got the thing translated. However much we owe the man, though, I cannot help being suspicious of all translations.

Possibly I was conditioned wrong as a child. In those days out in the Lariat country we had a town character, a grizzled and withered old man, who claimed to understand horse talk. Let a whinny sound from the stables, and the old man would cock his head and consider the sound for a moment.

"He says the weather is changing and that old bob-wire cut on his fetlock is hurting," the ancient would announce.

At an early age I began having doubts that this is what the horse said, but there wasn't any way of proving that he didn't say it unless you were another horse. This was not something that would lead one to a blind faith in translators.

On the surface you can't figure out any reason why a translator would put words in the mouth of some odd-ball poet, but it's easy to dig up some suspicious things.

I remember a translation from the Greek which went something like this: "When Phoebus ope'd the stables of the east and loosed his golden chargers in the sky." After some trouble and thought and retranslation, this roughly becomes "The sun rose."

It may be that that old Greek threw in all that extraneous stuff about Phoebus, though no self-respecting Dallas Greek would talk like that even if he did get up at sunrise. I have been in this writing business for a lot of years and this leads me to suspect that this particular translator had a rewrite-man complex. He had the feeling that he could always write something better than the man who wrote it originally. At times this practice has produced some passages you couldn't understand even if you *were* a horse.

Any old practitioner can spot what's happening in this Phoebus stuff right away. The translator is writing to protect himself. If he had written "The sun rose," somebody might pop up right away and say "Oh, no, it didn't." But nobody gives a hoot what Phoebus did with his horses.

Newspapers are faced with people all the time who want to back out of saying something even while they are saying it. One of the hardest jobs of a newspaper is to say what somebody else said in a way that he can't back out of.

Any politician will tell you that a man is always being misquoted when he is in a fit of anger or has had too much to drink.

Of course, all this is only what I suspect happened. It would be nice to know what Phoebus really did.

Sometimes the adults get pretty snotty about what they want the youngsters to read. Not long ago a lady librarian in Florida proposed that we junk all the Tom Swifts, Rover Boys, Ruth Fieldings, and other such books for kids. She said they were poorly written and empty of content.

The lady's mind has probably been poisoned by the sneaks who were always the villains in these books. Who wants content in a book, anyway? The average ten-year-old doesn't need it. He has content enough for three people himself. All he needs is an interesting plot, a stereotype, into which he can pour all that content and imagination, and he will provide his own reading experience.

I remember a book called *The Boy Scouts at Camp*. It came long before I ever joined the Scouts.

The characters in this book were so nonexistent that I don't even remember the names. The story was so trivial that the only memory of it is that somehow the Boy Scouts in camp caught a criminal. I have looked at the writing since and it is unbelievably bad, but at the time it seemed wonderful. Furthermore, the dialogue in the book was pretty sissified compared to the salty talk of our nine-year-old prairie world.

The content of the book was nil, but that wasn't the point. A small boy reading it personally went along on that trip. He helped pitch the tents. He savored that first evening meal and the talk around the fire later. He saw the moon come up over the lake and felt the clutch of the silent dark after the fire had gone out.

To this day it is a much more real camping trip than any I really made as a Boy Scout. These real camps turned out to be a lot of work, and some disagreeable things like getting soaked at the wrong time were always happening.

Also, the scoutmasters chickened out on hunting criminals. In all the time I was in the Scouts, you could count all the criminals we ever caught on the fingers of one hand or less.

In the same way, the other plays of Shakespeare are just plays of Shakespeare to me, but *Hamlet* is a living memory. I happened to read it at that age when for some hours a boy can be the Prince of Denmark, just as he actually is for a time Young Wild West, Jim Hawkins, that black-clad rider of the purple sage, Gluck, Tom Sawyer, Ishmael, Old King Brady, Will Drennan, or Tom Swift.

The reader who will be a reader all his life has to go through a time of insensate, indiscriminate reading. A boy at that time is full of himself. He has to spend himself on adventures of the imagination. The subtler satisfactions and rewards of reading come later.

My wife is friends with a second-grade sophisticate, a young woman seven years old. This young woman converses in two languages and in her seven years has already traveled in more countries than most people do in a lifetime. She spent the hot season reading all the Bobbsey Twins books.

Of such books is a reader made.

5

The Antique Virtues and Other Antiques

When I was growing up, it was common knowledge that any man was an utter and reckless fool to entrust his money to a bank when he could safely hide it in an old Wool Fat can among the Dr. Funston veterinary remedies in the harness room. Banks in those days were always "closing their doors." Everything would be going along famously, then suddenly it would be announced that the bank had closed its doors.

I had a relative who this way lost his entire savings account of ten dollars. It embittered him. Twenty years afterward, when I was grown, he was still complaining about it.

"I doubt," he said, "that I'll ever get back more than twenty-five cents on the dollar."

The country banks of those days were furtive places of shuttered doors, with blinds covering the windows. They seemed to stand in hostile aloofness among the gregarious general stores and barber shops and smithies.

It was our understanding that it was best to walk on

the edge of the sidewalk when passing and never to venture inside lest you come out without your pocketbook. The attitude of our people was generally that expressed on Ed Murrow's show by Clint Murchison when he said that you could do business with New York banks if you had enough collateral and enough eye teeth. Banks and the lawyers were the mortal enemies of financial well-being.

The first banker I can remember was an elderly man, cadaverous of face in a country where men were all weatherbeaten. He wore a black alpaca coat. The memory of him has the same stomach-muscle tone as the memory of Mr. Baker, the furniture merchant and undertaker. It seemed to a child that our banker constantly shied away to the edges of crowds, looking on them with a calculating suspicion. In those days he owned everything; anyhow, that is what we understood.

Occasionally we overheard the elders talking in hushed voices about some desperate man who owed a note at the bank. Nothing stirred my imagination again like the horror of this until I read that scene where Faust sells his soul to the devil.

There was a hint of the terrible about that sort of thing in those days. The man with a mortgage on his house was not only, on the face of it, recklessly improvident but probably also given to secret, expensive sinning. He risked not only financial ruin but the pits of hell.

As children, it was our understanding that his children became Little Match Girls and his widow had to sew for a living by lamplight into the early hours of the morning.

One would no more put a mortgage on his house than

he would buy a pound of steak from Mr. Schultz, the butcher, without watching what he did to the scales.

A man got his credit, if any, at the general store—maybe because if the store went bust the man didn't lose his farm. Even credit of this sort was suspect.

It was considered unwise to buy groceries on a thirty-day account. Our grocer was a kindly man. He was free with his jawbreakers and stick candy and sang a pleasant basso in church, humming most of the time and coming in with the words when he knew them. It was common knowledge around town, though, that he was bound to pad those thirty-day accounts. The bills always had more items on them than people believed they possibly could have bought.

The grocer undoubtedly spent some time selling merchandise, but it seems in memory that he spent most of his time trying to explain some five-cent item on a ticket that was already three weeks old.

Nobody went to the store and picked out his groceries. He got on the telephone and called in his order, and after a while an elderly man in a spring wagon clattered up with the groceries and deposited them in a crate on the porch.

Every family had a scale, a spring scale with a pointer indicator and a dial on the front, and it was religiously used on every package because it was commonly known that grocers shortweighted anybody that wasn't looking. If the sack of beans turned up two beans light, the lady of the house took time to dress in the formal manner required of downtown visitors and descended on the grocer with the sack and her own private scales to show him angrily how far he was off.

I once saw our grocer practically in tears over his inability to reconcile his scales with the numerous spring scales in town, no two of which agreed.

After a few years he got stomach ulcers, sold the business, and then began to complain loudly about the size of his grocery bills.

Of course, banks have changed. They are spacious, inviting places, and if you look at the TV bank ads any night you'll have trouble deciding what is mere merchandising and what is credit.

Almost everybody has a mortgage now, and somehow they have been made acceptable to religion. A friend of mine the other day said he never wanted to pay a house out. He would lose too much to time, revised zoning, and the weather unless he kept changing houses. He also said he never intended to buy an expensive appliance except on the installment plan.

"You've really got them when you need service," he explained.

A friend of ours who is building a new house almost revealed his age and the dark secret of his country upbringing when he first saw the plans.

"Where," he demanded, "is the front porch?"

His wife hushed him up before anybody noticed, but he still hasn't figured out where they are going to sit. As yet, he is only dimly aware that modern people have moved around to the back porch and started calling it a patio.

In my friend's day and my own, a back porch was not where you sat. After all, nobody would ever see you on the back porch. That was the place where you hung the steel traps.

The modern city householder would as soon be caught dead as be seen sitting publicly on his own property. He builds his front windows high so that the people on the street cannot see him, and he can't see them. There was a time in America, though, when you wanted to see somebody.

If you were a farm boy in those days, you sat by the hour in a family group on the front porch of the farmhouse, watching the wagon road and wishing someone would come by. You could watch a man's wagon crawl slowly from horizon to horizon, and before he disappeared, you would have learned from the adult talk about the fallacies of his farming practices, how he made out on his winter wheat and why he would never profit in a horse trade.

In those days sitting on the front porch required certain concessions to etiquette. Only the commoner people sat there in their undershirts and with their feet on the rail. One was supposed to be modestly dressed and to sit with both feet on the floor and behave. The kids in the porch swing were permitted to sway it gently, but there could be no pumping or other violent motion as long as the adults were around.

If a man walked by with whom the family was well acquainted, the father usually called out, "Going to town, eh, Jim?" That led to a long talk with a full explanation of his errand.

A nod and a polite greeting was all offered to a passer-by with whom you were not on close terms, though it was all right to speculate on what he was carrying home in that sack after he was out of hearing.

One of my most embarrassing moments came when I discovered that the front porch is known by various names around the nation. Most of us dimly realized that it was also the veranda. Once, after the family had moved to West Texas, I happened to call a front porch a front porch, and a new West Texas buddy hooted at the term.

"He don't even know the thing's a gallery," he told other acquaintances.

Probably the front porch has outlived its usefulness, but I hold with my friend against moving everybody around the house there to the back porch. Somebody is going to trip up on one of those steel traps.

Not long ago I took a peek into a railroad boxcar and discovered a shocking decline in American cultural activity. No boxcar art.

As a boy flunky at a Santa Fe depot, I had the chance to make a deep study of the bold outline murals that then decorated the walls of all but the most beat-up cars. There is no more inviting surface to the born artist than the smooth inner planking of a boxcar. For working it, you couldn't ask for better material than the black stencil paint or wax pencil ordinarily used for addressing boxes. All this fine stuff had thoughtfully been provided by the railroad out of its own pocket.

About the best of the boxcar murals there was a fresh

vigor and candor that we do not find in the works of people like Tom Lea or Peter Hurd. A boxcar artist, working before a sympathetic audience of only three or four, had no hesitation about drawing the division superintendent with saw teeth.

This kind of social protest furnished about half of boxcar art. One could detect in most of it a deep, underlying philosophy that lots of bosses were tightwads.

A good part of the other boxcar murals depicted hilarious scenes such as what went on around the office when the gang put a large-headed tack under the cushion of the billing clerk's chair. The only boxcar artist I ever knew specialized in these scenes and also in creating the incidents out of which he could make pictures.

He was a short, round man with cheeks as full as a squirrel's and an almost-constant malicious chuckle. It was not he who sent me all around town looking for red lantern oil, but he did send me walking a mile into the yards one day to seal a flat car. He it was who thought up the idea of calling the freight house after midnight on those freezing Panhandle nights. One of our force had to sleep there to handle emergency calls, and when the telephone rang, he had to walk half a block barefooted over icy timbers.

The best of this artist's pictures, though, didn't have to be set up. The apprentice telegraph operator came down one day the worse for drink and tried to climb the semaphore ladder with his feet up and head down. This picture was widely relished by the better railroad critics.

Very few boxcar artists drew women. They held it was unfair to include women in practical jokes.

The strain of serving as model for humorous pictures probably turned me away from railroading. I changed to a country newspaper. It did not matter that the boss immediately sent me around town hunting for a paper stretcher. By then, I was inured to injustice and lacked the talent to make pictures about it.

This study of boxcar art left its mark, however, in an extreme caution about biting at anything. I do not like to buy phonograph records, for instance. Who knows when the Edison cylinder record player with the diamond point needle will make a comeback.

A man named Spengler some years ago wrote a book called *The Decline of the West.* It is true that he spent most of his time in a garret and rarely came out to see the West decline, but he was obviously right. Things certainly aren't what they were when I was a boy.

Spengler thought up some good, sound, multiple-volume reasons for the West's decline, but he missed the real one. Behind the decline of the West is the decline of the school reader. If you have looked at one lately, you'll find it filled with Jane and Bill, ordinary uninteresting grade-school youngsters, who are shown adjusting in the right way to their community, their pets, their families and fellows.

I will admit that I started out on pap of this sort. My first hero, right out of what used to be called the Primer, was Faithful Dog Ned, a Newfoundland type who remembered so well a pat on the head given him by a little boy that he later saved the little boy from drowning. The point of this story was so moving that for several years I went around patting all dogs on the head at the risk of arms and rabies.

It was so moving to a younger brother that he conceived it his duty to round up the twenty or thirty stray dogs in town every day for breakfast, lunch, and dinner. Shortly thereafter Faithful Dog Ned ceased to be a family hero.

At any rate, Faithful Dog Ned wasn't typical. All the other books that used to be handed us at the beginning of the year were always put aside while I finished the reader. It was that fascinating. In my second-grade year, the reader was given over to Norse mythology. None of the Norse Gods was overly well adjusted to anything. Thor was actually a meathead and a common drunk, but a second-grader got nothing of that part of his character except his ability to drink an ocean out of his horn. Loki was a cheat and a swindler. The second reader skipped over their love life entirely. Still, nearly any boy or girl out of that second grade could give you today a pretty good character sketch of any god from that icy Pantheon.

Jane and Bill just aren't Thor. They make small lightning and thunder. And how compare their paltry adventures in the land of togetherness with the gilded enchantment of journeys to imaginary realms?

Those who remember the land east of the sun and west of the moon will know what I mean, and those who recall all the wonderful fictional characters from Rumpelstiltskin to Gluck of the Golden River. The fourth reader did so well with the Knights of the Round Table that Tennyson later seemed a little pale and Malory only a little more melodious. Do you remember the sprightly magic of *A Child's Garden of Verses* and the Christina Rossetti piece

about the bow that bridges heaven and overlooks the trees
and builds a bridge from earth to sky?

A reading experience came out of the old things that was
more than recognizing a word. It furnished the common
mental coin of western civilization, the vocabulary of myth
and metaphor and image common to all the varied languages. St. Nicholas transcended tongues.

Does anybody, by the way, have a copy of *The Rover
Boys in the Adirondacks?*

A school visit will quickly point up a further factor in
the West's decline. They no longer teach what in our
school days was called Expression, the art of expressing
fine moral sentiments in a belligerent voice.

This is a sad thing. It is sad to realize that nowhere in
this land is anybody being, in a loud voice, tired of planning and toiling in the crowded hives of men or longing for
the dear old river where he dreamed his youth away. It is
sad to know that nowhere is anybody energetically worrying about the old lady who was Somebody's Mother.

The United States may well rue the day it started its
youngsters to taking Jane and Bill to the farm instead of
teaching them that breathes there a man with a soul so
dead, etc. After all, it was in Expression that we learned
that the British soldier trembles when Marion's name is
told, and hardly any old vocal Expressionist is in doubt
about what Horatio did at the bridge.

In our day, Expression taught the tender twig patriotism,
thrift, and the love of Mother. He began with "Hats off! The
flag is passing by." By the time he had acquired the proper

stentorian tone, he had whipped off his hat so many times that the sight of a flag automatically started him whipping off his hat all the rest of his life.

This is undoubtedly the reason that President Eisenhower was bothered with bursitis.

Anybody who had any Expression at all once knew that he was captain of his fate, he was the master of his soul. He also knew that once or twice though you should fail, try, try again. He knew that whichever way the wind doth blow, some heart is glad to have it so, and if he preferred the Mike Hammer approach, he was aware that this is the law of the Yukon: That only the strong shall survive.

He preferred to live in a house by the side of the road and be a friend to man rather than having the oil fortune he has since got, and if Files-on-Parade said "What are the bugles blowing for?" he knew the answer. The fact that Byron once wrote a thing called "Address to the Ocean" wasn't hilarious in our set. We addressed the darn thing.

There were acres of diamonds everywhere in those days, and no date meant anything except four score and seven years ago. When duty whispered low, "Thou must," the youth replied, "I can."

Indeed, the whole art of thundering vocal appreciation seems to be fading away. We came on a Dallas lawyer friend at a moment when he was dissolved in unseemly mirth. The *Texas Bar Journal* had just carried a paragraph saying that "Mimeographed speeches suitable for lawyers to make before civic and school groups may be obtained upon request to the State Bar Secretary in Austin."

The Dallas lawyer said it was the first time he had ever heard of any lawyer without a few thousand well-chosen words to say on any subject that might come up.

This was so in the Lariat country. The lawyers most admired in my boyhood were those who could deliver a rousing speech even when they didn't know from moment to moment what they were going to say.

A lawyer once famous throughout the county visited our high school math class and was unexpectedly called on to say a few words in behalf of plane geometry. He looked a little dazed for a moment but brought the speech off handsomely. He went into detail to show that the ancient Greeks had thought well of plane geometry, and the Romans. He traced plane geometry through the Middle Ages and dared anyone to show that there had ever been a critical word said against it. By the end of the hour, he had got plane geometry down to the present, and he ended with a ringing declaration that any attack upon plane geometry was an attack on his personal honor. The class cheered and cheered.

Most of those old spellbinders had a single speech-making theme which they adapted to any subject.

The most admired defense attorney in the county was an elderly man who never tied his shoelaces and liked to squat on his heels in a chair instead of sitting. Mr. Davenport, as we will call him, was a specialist in making juries cry. In that West Texas day, when courtroom audiences turned on a lawyer's performance all the critical zeal that city people might devote to that of a fine actor, an ability to make a jury cry was much admired except when the jury included Mr. James Moore of our town. Mr. Moore cried at all the trials when he was on a jury. Mention that the prisoner was some mother's son, and Mr. Moore would start crying. The sight of him would inevitably start three or four other jurors into freshets, so he was regarded as unfair.

Mr. Davenport, though, could make a jury cry for a boot-legger from whom most of them had bought whisky. His main tool in this was Ingratitude More Strong Than Trai-tor's Arms. His speeches were full of serpents warmed in one's bosom and man's ingratitude that was sharper than a serpent's tooth; and many a hot July afternoon in the court-room resounded with his Blow, blow, thou winter wind! Thou art not so unkind, and so on and on.

Our best prosecutor in that time was a man who always began his speech with "I have prosecuted many but have persecuted no man," a statement repeated with some grim humor in our jail. Once the prosecutor ruined the Methodist Christmas-tree program, where he was dressed out as Santa, by absentmindedly beginning: "I have prosecuted many. . . ."

It is bad to see the legal profession moving into the gray flannel suit and the mimeographed speech.

One reason, probably, that we have got behind the Russians is that we have lost our regard for exact time. This nation has gone too much to the devil and to wrist watches.

It is easy to remember a time not so very long ago when a proper kind of man would as soon have been caught without his pants in public as with a wrist watch on his arm. Nobody but sports wore them. "Wears a wrist watch," the solid element of the community would say, mildly but in contempt of the man who affected one.

A man in those days wore a pocket watch roughly the size of the modern, degenerate live baseball. It was twenty-one-jeweled and properly adjusted. Those watches had beautiful yellow gold cases sometimes bearing pictures of hunting dogs and pheasants and prize fighters. Some of them had a little lid you could flip open with a careless flick of the thumb while you tilted your toothpick at a jaunty angle.

When a man ran into another timepiece, he immediately took his watch in the palm of his hand, compared the two and noted with pleasure how far the other man had got from the exact time.

The home companion piece to the pocket watch was the wall clock. When I was a child, two things about the household were absolutely forbidden to the touch of children. One was the shotgun on the rack over the fireplace and the other was the wall clock standing on a small high shelf.

The wall clock in any home was the exclusive concern of the paterfamilias. Women were not trusted to wind and regulate clocks.

Nine o'clock was bedtime in most homes then. It was more or less sinful to waste time by going to bed before that hour, just as it was morally questionable to keep late hours like nine-thirty or ten o'clock. Precisely at nine, the old man would appear from the bedroom, clad usually only in his long underwear, and walk with measured, purposeful steps toward the clock shelf in the living room.

"You kids be quiet," the mother of the house would command. "Papa is going to wind the clock."

The head of the house would carefully unlatch the little glass door at the front of the clock and pick up the big brass winding key from beneath the pendulum. Slowly, precisely, he would wind the clock the number of turns he had judged best for its mechanism. He would hold his watch in his hand and check the clock's face. Then he would blow out the light and go to bed, having imprisoned time for another twenty-four hours.

The first thing a man would do on entering the home of a friend was take out his pocket watch and check the time on the friend's wall clock. He didn't consider this being impolite. It was being careful. And a man with nothing else to do might take out his watch in midafternoon and take a critical look at the sun.

It wasn't that there was anything much to do with the time you had. It was just supposed to be exact.

In the same way, a train that was one minute late then wasn't "about on time"; it was late.

Yes, we started losing ground to the Russians when we got rid of the big gold watch chain and the Elk's Tooth watch fob.

A season or two ago we saw a lot of new evening clothes for men in Dallas at first nights of one thing and another, costumes with shirts with pleated fronts and ruffled cuffs and other things the like of which hasn't been seen since the day of his fat highness, the Regent.

I wasn't much impressed. For a long time, I have felt that men's clothing reached a peak of magnificence with the celluloid collar and has declined since.

The celluloid collar epitomized the style of dress that we used to see on the traveling drummers in Whitehorse Peters' barbershop in West Texas. Bored and worldly-looking men were these, with babyish skin on their faces instead of the saddle leather of the plainsmen, and with rich yellow gold fillings in their teeth.

All of us in the town knew, of course, that they were rounders, every one of them, with a probable history of sin that one could speculate upon for an hour.

No one since in my experience has been able to copy the lordliness of the gesture with which one of these men would unhook his celluloid collar with the tie inside it, hang the ensemble on a nail and then take his seat in the barber chair with both his gold collar button and his ennui at being cooped up in a small town showing.

The memory of this gesture is such that always after, when someone mentions the high and the mighty or the lords of creation, it is these men who come to my mind instead of the plutocrats with dollar marks on their vests and who were shown in the cartoons of our newspapers.

Their memory is redolent of the smell of the dozens of steamy towels slapped on faces after shaves and the vapors of heated witch hazel, camphor, and cologne. Anybody in a small plains town could sense a richness and a lavishness in the way that these men lived, and I determined to copy it when I got big.

Their style ran to such things as derbies in the winter and straw sailors with black grosgrain bands, worn at a jaunty angle, in the summer. The drummers wore the latest style of pegtop pants which flared around the hips and fit closely along the legs. Some had stickpins, and nearly every one had a conspicuous watch chain across the front of his vest with a proper fob advertising his fraternal order.

The key to the costume, though, was the celluloid collar. It gave a man a severely ordered look. It was about two inches deep all the way around and upheld the jowls and made everyone look a little long-necked. If a man wore his tie high enough, you could nearly always catch a glimpse of that testament to his affluence, the gold collar button.

By the time I had grown up and hoped to join it, this great day of men's fashions had disappeared. It is a lasting regret. All these years I have unconsciously been on the lookout for one of those great dressers. Occasionally, I spot an old-timer with a well-barbered look and that air of jaded worldly wisdom, and I think I have found one of the relics. Occasionally, he turns out to be a drummer, too, but that's about all.

Without the celluloid collar it isn't the same.

As man goes about finding more and more of his destiny in a pill, some sad things happen.

A man named B. G. Boshear at Grand Prairie, outside Dallas, was browsing through a grocery store and came across something advertised as "Old Fashioned Pound Cake." Having pleasant memories of pound cake, he bought one.

When he got home, though, he found out that his pound cake weighed only nine ounces. It turned out to be a gold pound cake, but Boshear was still disappointed. He was very naïve. The place to find a pound is not in a pound cake.

In recent years, the American people have worked out a revolutionary new system so that they can have a higher standard of living and eat more per person without gaining weight. Under this system, chicken salad is made out of tuna fish and tuna salad out of cheaper fish. Trout is not trout but flounder. The custard in custard pie is not custard but a kind of pudding. Beef may very well be calf. Certainly veal is. And I know a man who spilled a pint of milk on his new suit the other day, but the milk had some marvelous new kind of butterfat in it that didn't spot the cloth.

No, the pound cake is the wrong place to look for a pound. It would be better to look for it in a pint of something.

Out in West Texas my family once had a neighbor with as common a name as Jones, but he was never known as that. He was known as "the one with the bashful boy." It is a form of child worry that seems to have gone out of fashion now, but it used to be fairly common.

This particular bashful boy was called Will-yam, after the pronunciation used by his parents in yelling for him at top voice when anybody as strange as a cousin was around.

In school he seemed an ordinary enough little boy, only rather pleasantly secretive in manner and given to keeping himself apart from everybody else. It is true that he wouldn't answer questions in class. If the teacher tried to make him answer, he merely clamped his mouth tighter as if she were trying to get from him some information that he wasn't supposed to tell.

When you stopped at his farm home for a visit, though, all you saw of William in the beginning was one eye peeking cautiously around the corner of the house. This eye whisked out of sight the moment his father, a jocular man, started to separate the kids from the grown-ups. In a moment the father would be searching around the yard, saying, "Now where is that boy? *Will-yam* . . . WILL-YAMMM!"

A family hunt would then start, always unsuccessful, while William's father talked at length on the tribulations of trying to right up a bashful son and spunk him up a little.

William was possibly the only person who ever lived who had the ability to disappear on bare prairie.

On these visits it was always left to the children to track down William. I have hunted him a hundred times, searching behind the yucca stalks in the pasture, peering under the house, wandering down in the direction of the stock tanks. Once, after half a dozen of us had stood in the horse lot yelling for him for five minutes, I happened to look upward a few feet and discovered him crammed into a crevice of the loft above the granary. He was watching us silently. There was a long silence as we swapped looks.

"If you come up here," he announced quietly, "I'll knock your block off."

"Aw, come on down, Will-yam. Come on down and play."

The old routine followed. He didn't want to play. Go away. He didn't like us, so go home. He wished we would fall off the windmill tower. The thing to do with William when he was like this was stand there and keep quiet. Eventually, he would climb down and go along with you, warily keeping ten feet of space between himself and everybody else. As the hours passed, he would inch in closer and, finally, cautiously play a little.

Ever since, I have wondered from time to time what went on in his head.

The other day I visited with one of the boys from the old days, and we got to talking about a third-grade classmate who had moved onto a farm in the Pecos Valley near Fort Sumner and become a bachelor recluse. There would have been a poetic rightness about this if it had been William, but it wasn't.

William grew up to be a rather mean high school football lineman. He is now the manager of a small city chamber of commerce in West Texas, a greeter of people, deacon of his church, a toastmaster of some repute. Somewhere he found his own psychiatric lodestone.

Byron C. Dickinson, who used to live out in heaven and other points west, tells how Uncle Jim Jones once started driving back to his place near Tatum, N.M., after a visit to town.

He had to travel about five miles west on the Roswell highway before he turned north. The sun was in his eyes.

He had attended to some convivial duties while in town. Matter of fact, he still had some of the conviviality in a bottle, and his Model A was inclined to stray from one side of the road to the other. Presently he spotted another Model A approaching from the distance. It also was wandering from one side of the road to the other.

In the course of their zigzagging, the two cars managed to come together head-on in the middle of the road. The other driver crawled out. It was easily apparent that he might possibly have had a drink.

"Sorry," said the stranger apologetically. "All my fault. I wonder how much I owe you."

"Not at all," protested Uncle Jim. "I saw you comin'. Had plenty of time to take down the fence and get out of your way."

Uncle Jim wasn't being excessively polite. He was the sort of gentleman any old plainsman is familiar with. He was one of the good horsemen who came to grief with the horseless carriage back when the Model T was becoming the symbol of affluence but was certainly no substitute for a good horse.

One of my older friends in those days was an auto salesman named Bill Collins. He had sold one of the first Model Ts ever seen in the region to an old ranchman whom I remember as Zack.

About two or three hours after Bill had delivered the car and got back to town, a rider from the ranch raced into town on a horse foamy with lather. He had been ordered in, he said, to inform Bill that he had unloaded on Uncle

Zack a car that wasn't saddle-broke. Uncle Zack was in the car out in the north pasture but couldn't get it stopped. Bill was to get out there in a hurry and head it.

Bill jumped into his own Model T and sped to the ranch. He found the old rancher circling around in the pasture at a steady fifteen miles an hour, yanking back on the steering wheel and swearing mightily. By timing his jump right on the next trip around the circle, Bill made the running board and flipped off the brass ignition key. The old man blew out his breath as he let go of the wheel.

"Contrary-headed damn brute," he told Bill angrily.

Bill demonstrated the business of using those little old foot pedals to bring the car up short and showed the old man how to set the handbrake.

"All I ought to have to do," said Uncle Zack bitterly, "is drop the reins."

As I look back, it seems that there was a whole generation of these drivers. They were a marked breed. They eyed the road with grim-faced intentness. They gripped the steering wheel tightly, ready at any moment for the thing to shy or whirl. They drove with their white hats pulled down low over their eyes.

They had no heart for the horseless carriage at all, really. The only excuse for any kind of a carriage, by their lights, was the horse that drew it.

Miss Roberta Lavendar was a Virginia gentlewoman who looked every inch her name. Twenty years ago at the University of Texas, before bad health broke her, she was surely the best Latin teacher a beginner ever had. Sixtyish, tall and slender, white of hair, her bearing had pride and temper in it. Her face and eyes had the kind of inner beauty people used to call character.

She began each year by asking each new Latin student to pick up his text and turn to the vocabulary in the back. He was then told to grasp it firmly in his right hand.

"Now tear it out," she would order.

The vocabulary disposed of, she would fling a piece of chalk across the room and into a blackboard with a kind of zest.

"*Jacere; jacio, jeci, jactus,*" she began. "To throw; I throw. . . ."

So the class began learning Latin without grubbing for it. In a few weeks we were reading simple Latin; in a few months, Caesar. She communicated a kind of excitement to the task.

Of her students she demanded only rigorous study and a dauntless approach. To a student befuddled by a diagramming problem she would say imperiously, "Well, at least, get up and try."

Miss Lavendar had no use whatsoever for two things at the university—the school of education and the department of public speaking. She argued that a teacher should know something to teach and had the antique notion that a public speaker ought to have something of pressing import to say, an opinion that is obviously false because it is disproved in Dallas (and perhaps elsewhere) every day at the luncheon clubs.

I turned out to be the exception in her theory. I have always been afflicted with a voice that carries a mile at a shout but hardly more than two feet at normal volume. No middle ground. My mumbled recitations were an exasperation to her for two years.

"In all my years of teaching, I have never recommended that a student take a course in public speaking," she finally announced one day, "but you, young man, had better enroll in one."

Her teaching did not end in the classroom. She invented errands for her students to do, small favors to ask of them, so that she might talk and find out and shore up any real or fancied defects. She was intent on developing a whole person of each student.

She admired students who were poor in goods. She fancied they were fighting their way upward and onward against great obstacles, and many moneyless women students lived and worked at her house on Nueces Street in Austin over the years. She admired President Roosevelt extravagantly—not for his political views but because he was a handicapped man who refused to be a cripple.

Roberta Lavendar died in Austin a few years ago with few to say her an *ave atque vale.*

Most of us who studied under her sensed twenty-five years ago that Miss Lavendar's world was dying. It was a world in which learning was the beginning of wisdom, not the means for turning out supermechanics. To be able to read Latin was the mark of a gentleman, and a gentleman was one who would not stoop to do certain things, some of which are hardly looked upon today as mortal sins. To be a cultivated man was an end in itself. The measure of a man was his personal worth.

Perhaps it's just as well that all this died. It wouldn't work in the modern world.

All things antique get rarer with the passing years. The ash hopper has already disappeared. The fancy bedwarmer is about gone, with the mustache cup and the Gatling gun; and it is getting harder and harder to find an old-fashioned healthy person.

Most of us can remember when people were proud of being healthy and, if they were sick, they would hide it to enhance their reputations, but modern concrete-and-steel man's face wears only two expressions. It is either morbidly doleful as he concentrates on the things he feels wrong with his insides, or in times of relatively good health it is apprehensive over what is coming next.

I know advertising men who have set aside time every day to concentrate on their stomachs and see if they aren't getting ulcers; a writing friend, a man given to pills and doctors and reading books of symptoms, once had a morning of feeling suddenly wonderful. He rushed to a clinic in alarm and demanded a checkup, explaining that his nerves were steady, his sinus was dry, and his migraine gone.

"Now," he complained, "I don't even know what's wrong with me."

A man with neither ulcer nor migraine these days is a dull and colorless clod. In my West Texas youth it was different. I can remember hearing the older folk talk of young couples who were about to be married with the disapproving comment that one of them was "unhealthy." It was the same as saying that there was something shadowy about the youngster's family, or that he was a dead beat. Our family once had a distant woman relative who had what was called the lingering sickness. People were kind to her, but they felt somehow that she had let the family down.

It was the thing to be healthy, and even people who weren't would say they were. Our town had a Civil War veteran once, a man in his middle nineties who could neither see, hear, nor think very well any longer, whose contribution to any conversation was a sturdy "Feelin' fit as a fiddle" repeated at intervals.

Only gunshot wounds, broken bones, and snakebites were worth going to the doctor about then. A good round of calomel or a dose of Black Draught would cure anything else.

Modern man has become a strange sight, a kind of walking boundary for a population of germs. His sinuses stream freshets. His ulcer eats like the Spartan fox. His high-pressured blood sounds with great swishes against his eardrums as it foams through his hardening arteries. His feet are flat, his eyes see through yellow and green spots, and at night when he lies awake and thinks hard on it, he can sometimes detect a heart flutter or the beginning of a kidney stone.

And now, if you'll excuse me, I'll be getting out of here. I'm not feeling so good these days.

6

If the Alaskans don't like it here, why don't they go back where they came from?

At indecently short intervals the United States passes around another joke on Texas. The latest one concerned a Texan who went to Heaven and found nobody singing Hallelujah, in fact no singing of any kind. The singing angels had been sent off on another mission.

As any Texan would, this one decided to do something about it. He approached Saint Peter.

"Let's organize a choir of hymn-singers," he said. "I want a thousand sopranos, a thousand tenors, and a thousand contraltos."

"Well," said Saint Peter, "I think I can furnish them, but what about the bass?"

"Oh," replied the Texan, "I'll do the bass myself."

This restrained estimate of Texan capabilities was supposed to be funny all over the country, but we have to ask the gigglers of the other states of this Union: Who has been singing bass around here for the last few years?

All this provoked some research on why Texas is supposed to be funny, most of the research having been done in the brain of Mr. Frank King, the retired Associated Press tycoon and Texas newspaper mogul. Mr. King has traveled all over, from Cathay to the Indian Nations, and he has the theory that people laugh about Texas because it's the only thing left in the United States strong enough to stand being laughed at.

Texas, of course, can stand anything. It does, every year.

You can't laugh at the other states or cities or they will get mad. As a state, California is sensitive and has a right to be. Anybody who has ever seen Philadelphia knows that it is no laughing matter. Florida is a few fauna and flora entirely hidden by New Yorkers on vacation; when the alligators spot the first visitors arriving, they run off into the swamp and hide.

If you josh Oklahomans a little, they bring up that football team. Until Alaska came along, Arkansas was about the only state left with which we could swap a little foolery, the only place where people understood what one was about and replied in kind. Of course, an Arkansas laugh just isn't as big as a Texas laugh, and the Alaskan laugh has a northern accent.

You just can't laugh at people any more. The dialect story is out. Stories about races and creeds are bootleg items. Only the Irish have not laid down the law, and the Irish joke has been damaged because people have found out that Pat and Mike were not really Irishmen. All Irishmen are named Sean.

This leaves Texas as the thing United States people can laugh about without looking over their shoulders or lowering their voices.

It is one thing to laugh about the Texan who was going to sing bass in the heavenly choir, but people around the nation have been guffawing at a lot of other Texas stories that didn't actually happen. These stories are by-products of a strange phenomenon: The people of other states have invented a wholly mythical Texas and proceeded to make war on it. It was unnecessary and hardly seems fair, as Texas has the rest of the country outmanned. An odd offshoot of this false image-making is the fact that Texas things and people, when they leave the state, seem to expand in size.

Whenever one of those magazine writers comes down to get the big Texas story, one of our rich men takes him off and lets him photograph some money. This so impresses the writer that he rushes off and does a piece about solid-gold Texas. The magazine writers haven't caught on yet that they're all seeing the same old hundred-dollar bills.

Let a Texan happen to mention outside the state that he has a little old hundred-section ranch, and the outlanders immediately blow it up into a 640,000-acre spread.

"This character," says one of them, "has a 640,000-acre ranch. Boy, how exaggerated those Texans are!"

The true Texan, of course, always understates things. If you don't believe it, take a look at the figure he gave for his income on his last income-tax return.

Every Texas figure grows at least three zeros behind it whenever it pops up outside of Texas. Piper Cubs become B–36 bombers in out-of-state talk. A Texan's boot heels

rise at least an inch the minute he steps off Texas soil—
and his corns hurt twice as much.

Texas gamblers go to New York and inflate into society
figures. Back in the evil old days in Dallas I knew a minor
dice man who took a trip to Los Angeles. He started out
of Dallas with a Lincoln Continental and maybe six thousand dollars. By the time he reached the coast, his hold-
ings had increased to 150 oil wells, two refineries, two big
cattle ranches, an island in the Gulf of Mexico, and a
date with a movie queen.

This is the way a lot of Texas fortunes are born.

This is not to say that there aren't Texans with an al-
mighty amount of money. These Texans have almost as
much money as the rest of us Texans don't have. When
a bank cashier runs off with a hundred thousand dollars
down in the heart of Texas, you usually will find one man
wondering how much money he took and two hundred
fifty wondering whether he happened to destroy the over-
drafts.

The people around the country will believe any silly
figure about Texas if it has nine zeros after the front
number, but they are always shocked at Midland Man
and horned toads and other items in the Texas that does
exist. When Midland Man was discovered, even the
Smithsonian Institution got excited and started spouting
about how Midland Man was even older than Folsom
man. It said, with exclamation points, that Midland Man
was twelve thousand years old.

Most of us down here in Texas failed to see what all

the excitement was about. Something about the sunbaked, dry air in West Texas mummifies the body and invigorates the spirit. Out there the human carcass is seared quickly on all sides so that the inner juices are preserved. On the high baldies there are characters practically twelve thousand years old still walking around, and how does the Smithsonian get away with calling a West Texan of these moderately ripe years a fossil anyway?

It has not been a year since the newspapers in the East sprouted headlines because some government wildlife expert announced that the horned frog really can squirt blood out of its eyes.

This was all very well, but who said it couldn't in the first place?

A lot of foolish folklore is going around about horned frogs. Supposedly sensible naturalists say that the frog is able to squirt blood because fear causes a rupture in a sinus at the corner of the eye. This is superstition. Actually what happens is that the frog squints an eye and lets fly. Anywhere the blood hits you it will cause a wart. Everybody in West Texas knew this from experience, just as everybody knew that the horned frog has remarkable staying powers. It is only outlanders who doubt.

Most of the nation was skeptical about Old Rip, the horned frog who lived sealed up for forty years in the cornerstone of the courthouse at Eastland, Texas, for instance. The foreign cynics claimed that a horned frog cannot live forty years in a cornerstone.

This is nonsense on the face of it. The horned frog has no sense of time. If you put him in a cornerstone and then take him out forty years later, how does he know whether he has been there forty years or not?

The outlanders say the frog couldn't have breathed. So far as Texans know, nobody has ever attempted to prove that the horned frog breathes.

Any boy of my generation knows about his food habits. If we were not fishing in those days for tarantulas, we were tending a pen of horned frogs and trying to find out what they ate. We fed them everything—ants, mosquitoes, flies, grass, woodseeds, vanilla extract, and chewing tobacco. Yet they all died.

It wasn't until years later that somebody realized the truth: *The horned frog does not eat.* If the horned frog does not eat, it seems hardly necessary for him to breathe.

At any rate, the people of other states could profitably devote all their conversational time to *legitimate* Texas topics.

When the *Big D* column was still teething, Mr. Harlan Miller, the Des Moines columnist, rhetorically queried his readers in the following vein:

"Will the proud brags of Iowans dominate the world's next fifty years as the deafening boasts of Texans have dominated our last fifty?" He went on to imply that they would.

This sort of remark is typical of the misconceptions so rampant about Texas. In the first place, Texas boasts are not deafening. They are carefully kept just short of that so they will have maximum effect.

In the next place, there isn't anything wrong with the

volume when an Iowan brags; it's the subject matter. Nobody can run a bluff if he hasn't actually the chips to back it up. One look at Texas will convince anybody that anything can happen there and probably did, whereas it is hard to see how anything ever happened in Iowa.

Mr. Miller said that third-rate Texas hotels were full of oil millionaires sitting in thirty-dollar-a-day rooms and trying to find out how to spend their money. Actually, of course, they are in Reno and Las Vegas keeping up the state of Nevada.

Mr. Miller was trapped into several other errors. Of Texans he went on: "They made their noisiest money in oil, and that's something like winning it in a crap game. ... Money made in corn and hogs and insurance and farm mortgages is likelier to be strong, silent money." Money made in corn and hogs these days, of course, is likelier to be government money. Mr. Miller continued: "You can take a kernel of corn off a five-foot Texas stalk and plant it in Iowa soil, and it grows thirteen feet tall." Possibly. It depends on where a person looks for the ear. Texans have always looked down on corn while Iowans seem to have the habit of looking up at it.

"You can see a man selling cotton candy at the Iowa State Fair or hawking Twenty-three Skidoo lapel buttons and where is he from?" asked Mr. Miller, taking a rhetorical stance. "Dallas, Texas, naturally."

This charge is unfortunately true.

Iowa is about the only place left where you can sell Twenty-three Skidoo buttons, and a man who has gone broke on his fifth dry hole has to have some place to raise another stake.

Mr. Miller was amused that Texans would pay forty or sixty-five thousand dollars for an Iowa bull, but when a Texan is out on the town there's no telling what he will buy.

Iowans are wonderful people, but they will never succeed at bragging because they have no genius for authentic lying.

In this, however, they are not inferior to most of the rest of the world. Somebody sent me a copy of a book called *Arizona Brags,* by Oren Arnold. In it he told of a sandstorm so thick out there that a prairie dog was seen digging a hole fifty feet in the air. This shows one reason Texas stays so far ahead of the other states. None of them ever swipes anything from us until it is worn out. I know for a fact that that prairie dog was up in the air in West Texas fifty years ago. At that time he was trying to get down, realizing he had overworked the gag.

At times it seems that the people of the lesser states resent without reason the Texans' status as chosen people. They seem to blame the Texans themselves for this.

It seemed to us down here, for instance, that there was a great deal of smug satisfaction around the country during the last presidential campaign because the Texan on the Democratic ticket had to run in second place.

Some Texas people got pretty irritated at Lyndon Johnson. They figured that if he couldn't run the United States he ought to have nothing to do with it. It is easy to see now, though, that Senator Johnson took on the hardest job of the campaign. All John Kennedy had to do was run for President. Senator Johnson faced the task of restraining himself into second place.

He did it, too. He squeezed all of himself into second place, and to elect John Kennedy he went all out—even to Massachusetts. Lyndon went up there and shook whatever Yankee hands were not holding on to their pocketbooks and ate a serving of beans and praised the codfish industry.

When he came back to Texas, he announced that he had gone up to Massachusetts as a Texan and that the people up there had been real nice to him. Since the people of other states are hardly ever sufficiently appreciative of a Texan, this caused the Texans to warm to Mr. Kennedy immediately.

When Kennedy came to Texas, Senator Johnson and Sam Rayburn steered him past the Texas pitfalls carefully. They kept him from riding in any Cadillacs. A Texan may own three Cadillacs himself, but he does not like his candidate to ride in one because it shows others that he lacks the common touch. Mr. Kennedy was kept from wearing any clothes with a perfect crease in them while he was in the state. The Texan acts politically out of instinct rather than reason. When he sees a city-dressed politician, he is likely to glare at the candidate and think to himself, "There he goes in his $150 suit with all the creases in it, with his homburg and his beauty-shop haircut and his dinky mustache. Thinks he's smart, does he? I'll get me a ballot and show him."

Somehow word got around Texas that the Kennedys probably owned some oil wells somewhere, and this didn't hurt John Kennedy either. Mr. H. L. Hunt, the fabled Texas wildcatter, even issued a letter stating that he had detected no signs of fiscal irresponsibility in the Kennedy family.

Nor was the Kennedy cause hurt any when the ugly rumor got out that Henry Cabot Lodge diets. Imagine!

Not that this last had anything to do with Senator Johnson's struggle to accommodate himself to second place. Anyhow, he did a good job, but we fear the country as a whole is too envious properly to appreciate it.

Some time back a seventh-grade girl whose dad was stationed at Randolph Field in San Antonio wrote to some officials of the state of Georgia for dope to "prove Texas is not the best state in the Union."

She thought Georgia might be—never having seen it, of course.

Anyhow, this so tickled the Georgia House of Representatives that it voted through a resolution offering her refuge on the grounds that the official to whom she had written "fears for her safety while located among Texans during this crisis."

It tickled the papers over that way, too, and they made much of it, hoping to discomfit the Texans.

Actually, it just showed what had been proved before.

Anybody of seventh-grade attainments can get the Georgia legislature to pass almost anything.

One gets the idea that the foreign scribbler and the foreign politician are lying in wait, hoping that Texas will slip up so they can pounce. Back when we were having that argument about tidelands oil, things got especially bad. When the Senate voted the quit-claim bill that gave Texas its tidelands ten leagues to sea, Columnist Ollie Crawford of the Philadelphia *Inquirer* wrote that the Senate had put part of the deep in the heart of Texas.

He said that twenty per cent of the fish in the Gulf of Mexico were entitled after that to wear ten-gallon hats.

This is the kind of thing that goes on all the time. In this instance, Mr. Crawford ignores the fact that the fish of the Texas coast are Texans by birth and temperament.

The tarpon, for instance, is obviously a Texan. Like other Texans, he is a trusting, friendly soul; and he often gets hooked by some outlander. When this happens, the tarpon, in typical Texas fashion, calls attention to himself. He rises in the air like a rocket and dances on his tail while the blue mist shines around him. He looks ten times as big as he is. A tarpon out of the water is just a white fish, but while he is putting on the act, he glows with the colors of rainbows. He weighs a hundred pounds and pulls like a ton, and he keeps this up until the outlander is usually sorry that he started the whole thing.

When the tarpon gets good and ready, he shrugs his catch off with a slight curl of the lip and departs to chase a whale off his tidelands.

Something about the stern New England conscience seems to be bothered when you mention food. I once jotted down a piece about a Connecticut restaurant that was advertising "Southern Fried Chicken—New England Style," and it angered all the New Englanders in the North Texas countryside. Mrs. John Fox, for instance, declared that the New England kind of Southern fried chicken could be no worse than some "Yankee pot roast" she had got at a Dallas restaurant. It was served with a cornbread dressing.

"Horrible to contemplate is right," declared Mrs. Fox, with three exclamation marks at the memory.

Another lady wrote: "Being a Connecticut Yankee myself, I think it is my duty to inform you that Southern Fried Chicken—New England Style is no worse than Coney Island Hot Dogs—Texas Style.

"Furthermore, just what don't you like about New England cooking? Some of the things that Texans manage to cook up would discourage a cannibal. Let's use a little more tact when speaking of New Englanders and their cooking. Yours truly. . . ."

Tact is hardly the word for it. Utter quiet is the policy to follow at this point unless you want to get invited to a New England boiled dinner.

The human animal is sensitive to remarks about what he eats. You can say whatever you like about what he drinks or the clothes he wears and he will probably let it pass.

Even if he is eating pigs' feet, however, he wants you to understand that he is eating high on the hog.

New Orleans people, for instance, have a kind of shellac syrup which they have mistakenly identified as coffee. It is made by extracting all the water out of the coffee. A sip of this stuff will cause the stranger's eyes to bug from their sockets. It also causes hair to grow out from under the fingernails and the teeth to fall out.

Any New Orleansian can sip this stuff, though, and deliver learned comments on the blending of mocha and Java and the Brazilian green. As a result, New Orleans people never sleep from Wednesday until Saturday. They go to parties.

They do not take kindly any slighting references to this brew, either. In the same way, people who live mostly on cabbage don't like you if you fail to appreciate the cabbage.

Ever since that first *faux pas* I have tried to say something good about New England food, however hard it is.

A good thing to eat in New England is vegetables. In that soil, vegetables live a strenuous life. They get muscled up, more or less, as they never do in softer soils. A New England potato, for instance, is spare and gaunt and full of tasty juices.

And anybody can write a great prose poem on the virtues of the Maine lobster. As food, he is pure gold—especially after you have paid the shipping costs on him all the way to Texas.

In the war between the states, as I have been involved in it now and then, two states keep coming back to the skirmish line—Oklahoma and California.

With Oklahoma this is easy to understand. On any given day its people are all in Dallas, Texas, where they are likely to protest at any time. Oklahomans are a fine, wonderful people—given, like Texans, to chastising the infidel and fighting over governors. Texans and Oklahomans have fought, bled, and died together even when there was nobody else to fight. Even if this were not true, a Texan would have to be on Oklahoma's side. If there were no Oklahoma, there would be nothing on the north of Texas, and it is unthinkable for Texas to have a side on which it has nothing to be better than. Oklahoma serves a function. Texas is gigantic, of course, but it has to stop somewhere, and stopping short of Oklahoma is about right.

Oklahomans do not understand this. When the Department of Commerce published a booklet called "General Characteristics, Oklahoma," somebody remarked that it was a waste of the taxpayer's money. Everybody already knew the characteristics of Oklahoma—size, speed, deception, good blocking, and so on. All this was in good, clean fun, but it produced an uproar. It seems hard to say anything these days about Oklahoma that doesn't hit home.

It is harder to understand how California, crushed once to earth, keeps coming back. Probably Californians have an uneasy feeling that they have something that belongs to Texas. Texas captured California—as well as the Arctic Circle—from Mexico in the Texas Revolution. After the Mexican War, Texas gave California to the United States to get rid of Pershing Square and to allow the United States to develop the sequoia and redwood forests. If

Texans had turned up with trees as big as those, they would never have been believed.

Mention that something new has been developed in Texas and some California son of the Golden West is always ready to rise and sneer "Hick stuff! We invented that before the Russians."

California is a place of vague uneasiness, disquiet, fearful expectancy, and widely circulated warnings about things that haven't been invented yet. It is a great center of research in such things as A-bombs, windbroken race horses, and earthquakes, none of which have probably happened. Half the plagues of the nation have been thought up to fulfill some California fear.

As we remember it, a San Francisco newspaperman scooped the nation on the 1929 crash. He ran into it the day before it happened.

Some biologists out there caught a mouse and put it in a cage with a rattlesnake. They were going to study the rattlesnake's method of eating the mouse. The mouse quickly killed the snake. It seemed to make the whole state jittery. All that happened, apparently, was that they happened by accident to get hold of an old-time West Texas mouse, a fierce animal which had nothing to eat except rattlesnakes after the bison were killed out in West Texas. Nobody knows why the old-time West Texas mouse was so pugnacious. Probably it was because there wasn't enough water out there for both people and cats, and the mouse grew up without fear. In recent years the mouse in West Texas seems to have softened up a lot, having been exposed to the cultural but debilitating influences of fiddle music and painted houses.

The anti-Texas rebellion reached a kind of high point when Alaska came up for statehood. Glee naturally was unbounded all over the country at the thought of having Texas surpassed in size.

California was in there fast.

The Los Angeles *Mirror News* ran an exulting two-column editorial.

"Texas would automatically become the No. 2 state in size, which would deprive Texans of their Topic A in bar conversation," declared the *Mirror News* writer.

Next time you see a Texan in a bar take a look around. You will notice that a Texan in a bar seldom wastes time in conversation about anything. It is the Californians who insist on talking when it is inappropriate.

It happened that Texas had already made the acquaintance and taken the measure of Alaska in a kind of scouting attack. Some of us had pointed out that Alaska was mostly a figment of imaginations at work up there during those long winter nights. This seemed to stir the whole Territory to anger. A warming stream of epithets began to arrive by mail at my desk along with gifts of moose steaks, beaded moccasins, and small totem poles. Letters still smelling of the dog teams began coming in from the entire population of six or eight, and the Fairbanks *News-Miner* got downright personal.

It ran a piece which concluded with "Crume does not pay."

This was something that the creditors had known all along, but there was no point in dragging it out in public.

The *News-Miner* made some slighting remarks about the state in general, too. It quoted somebody from Fort

Worth as saying "Book learning, like culture in general, is so new to Dallas that literacy in any form is to be commended."

The state of culture in Fort Worth is such that it habitually has a fine football team and doesn't even know it. Culture in Alaska, of course, consists of the Montgomery Ward catalog.

A man named Rex Holman from Homer, Alaska, an occasionally noticeable settlement in the fog, claimed over the airwaves: "We have king crabs here that will measure twenty-four inches across the back. I know Texas has some awfully big crabs, but I doubt very much if they can come up with something bigger than this."

It should be obvious that Mr. Holman knew nothing of the history of the Texas Gulf and did not know that the Texas whaling industry was killed out by crabs which ate up the breeding stock.

What happened when Alaska came into the Union? Nevada got mad because it was no longer the most sparsely settled state. Dallas and Houston, Texas, moved into the Kenai oil fields along with part of Tulsa, Oklahoma, and they and the Alaskans have been pounding each other on the back and telling big windies and pulling practical jokes on each other ever since.

Actually Texas is an admirer of Alaska. It is nice to be able to associate with somebody our own size for a change.

There are only a few minor things wrong with Alaska, and it was inevitable that hospitable Texas folk would tell them how to straighten things out. No matter what our friends on the *News-Miner* say, for instance, Alaska basically is a state that has spread itself too thin. It would have progressed faster if it had concentrated some place.

People have argued that there is just as much of nothing in the Big Bend of Texas as there is in Alaska. There is a difference, however. In the Big Bend, nothing is all squeezed up close together. In Alaska, nothing has been allowed to run wild.

Alaska runs to foolish exaggeration in a lot of things. Bears, for instance. Alaska produces one-ton bears, which is a useless and silly practice. A five hundred-pound bear is enough.

And Alaska has mountains you can't climb, so what's the point of them?

In a lot of things, however, Alaska and Texas are complementary, and they can help each other out. Alaska, for instance, has spectacular scenery everywhere but no roads to get to it. Texas has virtually all the fine highways in the world, but a lot of them don't seem to be going any place.

Also, the main Alaskan industry is producing gold for Fort Knox.

Any Texan will tell you that gold is compatible to him. The average Alaskan has so much gold that it is practically worthless, and it is beneath his dignity to fool with anything that costs less than ten dollars. Chewing gum priced at less than that is looked upon as inferior stuff. The Alaskan, however, is often short on onions, and I have known them to sell in Nome for a fortune per onion.

Texans, on the other hand, are shorter on pure gold than they would like to be, but when it comes to onions

—especially late in the season on a wet year—they are often stinking rich.

I once knew a typical wealthy Alaskan. He lived in a thriving community consisting of his house, the Russian church, and a trading post about a thousand miles from the nearest telephone.

He farmed foxes on an island he had rented from the government and owned the only big black Cadillac in Alaska, for all I know.

He always spent the summer months living it up in the fine hotels of San Francisco and Seattle, to which he had gold-crusted credit cards. Sometime each summer he would marry a new wife. Along in September, when the snowline had begun creeping down from the peaks, they would ride into his home town on a ship. Soon the gales would begin, and he would be safely married until some other ship could fight its way into the harbor.

The wives arrived looking excited about a life of money with a Cadillac but departed on the first ship that could get in. It isn't much fun to ride around in a Cadillac if there is nobody to see you, especially if there is only a mile or so of road it can travel on.

Possibly this makes our wealthy Alaskan sound eccentric. Whatever else he was, he was an amiable man. When he was around the island, he was always generous with his money and would let you carry around a few thousand of it for several days if you wanted to.

The nation has missed the whole point and spirit of the Texas tall talk, because it has insisted on talking instead of listening. Outlanders never understand that the Texas tall talk is not a lie. It is the expression of the larger truth. At its most trivial, it is a tale made up by a Texan out of the goodness of his heart to entertain his friends from other states, or maybe just to improve the shining hour.

For example, there was the man who stalked into a drugstore in Comanche, in West Texas. He was about six feet four inches tall by the estimate of Walter J. Cunningham, who told me about it. The stranger weighed about 240 and wore a gigantic cowboy garb, including a tent-sized hat and riding boots the size of a child's saddle.

"Give me the strongest drink you have. Carbolic acid, if possible," he thundered as he bellied up to the soda fountain.

The puzzled soda jerk finally produced a small Coke. The man took a drag at it and cleared his throat.

"I rode a tiger into town," he announced, "which I caught in the mountains near my home, and I used a rattlesnake as a quirt."

He finished his drink with another gulp.

"And," he added, "I was run out of Blanket, Texas, because I was a sissy."

This clearly isn't any plain lie. It has a solid core of something you can't quite put your finger on.

This is typical of the sort of thing the Texan whips up between oil-well fires when time hangs heavy on his hands. Actually, the Texas stories he relishes himself are more nearly comments on the wry nature of the Universe. They told a story, for instance, about the Reverend S. B. McKeown, an early-day minister who wandered into a

West Texas region when the ranchers were trying to keep the farmers out. It was also a time of a big drought.

"All this country needs is a little more water and a few good men," the minister observed one day to a rancher.

"Yeah," said the rancher. "So does hell."

And J. Evetts Haley, the historian, tells a story about the late Charles Schreiner of Kerrville. In his last years, the old rancher had a chauffeur to drive him in a limousine around his ranches, but he loved the cattle business and he loved chuckwagon food—a food that was not universally admired.

One day, after Schreiner had stopped at a camp for a chuckwagon lunch, one of the cowboys gazed at the departing limousine.

"If I had as much money as that old so-and-so," he said, "I'd live on nothing but canned goods for a month."

Far from being big lies, these stories are all less than the Texas truth. It is a matter of record that an Army captain got into a poker game and drinking bout in old Mobeetie, during which he shot and killed an enlisted man after a drunken quarrel.

The ensuing court-martial found that the captain did indeed kill the soldier and that he had broken regulations by playing poker with an enlisted man in the first place. However, the court acquitted the captain of the killing on the grounds that, under the circumstances, it was the only dignified thing he could do.

It is this down-to-earth quality about Texas that outlanders just never appreciate.

The Texan is expert at another form of japery better

understood by mere people. It is practiced by citizens of all the states, but the Texan's rich imagination and instinctive talent for private enterprise get a chance for full play.

A few years ago a dairy farmer near Comanche, Texas, began to be bothered by people, always old and ailing people, who were coming on his land. He found out that somebody had gone over the farm with a Geiger counter and found enough uranium in the soil to make a click or two. At the time there was a lot of talk about radiation healing, and the visitors wanted permission to come on the farm and sit in the soil in the hope that it would remedy their various ailments.

After a few months, the dairy business was swamped. The farmer finally built a shed over some of the sand and put some wooden benches in it. He put up a sign saying that he didn't claim that the uranium would cure anything and began charging a small admission fee.

The shed had been full of patients for days when two secretive old men came up with a glint in their eyes. One had a stump of a leg where his left foot should have been. They paid their fee, went back in the shed to a bench by themselves, took off their shoes and thrust their feet in the dirt. For fifteen or twenty minutes, they sat there while the other patients concentrated deeply on their hurts.

Suddenly the old man pulled the stump of the leg out of the dirt and thrust it into the air.

"My god," he yelled. "Look what it did to my foot."

The crowd almost exploded. It all but tore down the sides of the shed getting out. Lame men who had not walked in years suddenly found themselves sprinting. People of short breath were half a mile away before they found they were tiring.

Nobody knows what became of the one-footed man. He escaped before anybody found a noose.

My favorite practical joke of this kind, however, was engineered by Mr. John Fitzhugh. Mr. Fitzhugh is now a courtly man of near eighty, a person of gentle manners, generous instinct, and bubbling good humor. For years, he was public-relations director of the Santa Fe Railroad out of Galveston.

Many years ago he and another railroad man were killing a stormy, rainy April afternoon with some drinks in a hotel room at Temple. Freshets of water would periodically drop from the sky. The rain would stop for a few minutes and hail would rattle on the roof. Between hailstorms, they could see people in the street below picking up the hailstones and measuring them.

The two men went to the hotel basement and bought a hundred-pound cake of ice. They borrowed a hatchet and chopped off the corners of the cake until it was approximately round. Then they carried the ice to the hotel room and poised it on the window sill. When the next spate of rain and hail hit, they pushed the ice ball out into the air. It fell on the lawn below with a spectacular splat and half-buried itself in the mud.

People began waving excitedly and sprinting for shelter. From windows across the street, they stood watching the giant hailstone.

This had been going on for thirty minutes when suddenly an old car roared up and skidded to a stop. Two men jumped out and ran toward the ball of ice. Mr. Fitzhugh recognized them as a reporter and a photographer from a daily paper in Waco, twenty miles away. Gulling the press was no part of his joke, and he hurried down to head them off.

By the time he had got to the street, the photographer was shooting pictures as fast as he could change plates. The reporter was dashing around in excitement, waving his hands. Mr. Fitzhugh kept tugging at his sleeve and telling him, in a low voice, that the giant hailstone was a fake.

The reporter suddenly turned on him in fury.

"Don't tell me it's a fake," he shouted. "I see it with my own eyes."

It seemed time to retreat temporarily. Mr. Fitzhugh did. Next morning the paper came out with the story and pictures of the hailstone on the front page.

For years, Mr. Fitzhugh worried at times about the hoax, but he could never find an appropriate moment to confess to the newspapermen. Thirty years later he dropped by the newspaper and found the reporter still there, though he was now a desk man with a newspaper lifetime behind him. Mr. Fitzhugh brought the talk around to the subject gently.

"Remember that giant hailstone?" he asked.

"Best story I ever covered," said the newspaperman, and he began to retell it enthusiastically.

Mr. Fitzhugh listened to it and then slipped quietly away.

That was four or five years ago. He has never been back.

So, if you read in the record books that a hailstone weighing in the neighborhood of seventy pounds once fell in Temple, it isn't a Texas tall tale. But it wasn't a hailstone either.

Several years after everybody in Texas had already announced it, a Harvard anthropologist named Dr. Evon Z. Vogt made a study and discovered that Texans really are different. Anyhow, it was reported that way in the *Science News Letter*.

Dr. Vogt discovered that Texans are highly competitive people who make a lot of noise about it and that they like to ball the jack when work is to be done and then do positively nothing for a while.

There is doubt that this part of the study is exactly accurate. It would be more accurate to say that Texans prefer at all times to do positively nothing. However, they have to work hard most of the time to pay the enormous rentals on their many safe-deposit boxes.

As for being competitive, Texans have always believed in the theory of may the best man win—which is merely enlightened self-interest.

Actually, these are awfully measly ways for Texans to be different, but we are all grateful to the doctor for proving scientifically what anybody can see with the bare eyeball.

Almost anybody could think of several bigger ways that Texans are different. There! We have finally got in the key word. There is something in the Texas soil which produces men of big physique and a certain largeness of narrative and descriptive powers.

The original Texas Indians along the Gulf Coast were all eight or ten feet tall. Some people believed that these Karankaways got their great size from the Gulf oysters they ate. The oysters were naturally of the giant variety. Long after oysters and Indians both disappeared, however, the trend in Texas continued upward like modern stable prosperity. During the longhorn cattle days of Texas history, it was believed that Texans got their great physical and mental powers, to say nothing of their vocabulary, from eating beef that was free of the debilitating fat found in the beef from Iowa and the other midwestern states.

In recent years, some northerners have argued that Texans grew to a great height from constantly looking down their noses at the financial assets of other states.

Probably none of these is wholly true. There is just something in the Texas soil which produces big men, usually even without water.

Great as the Texan's physique may be, of course, it is as nothing to the grandeur of his mind. At the whittler's bench in any small Texas town you can find at any hour of the day a man who can take a dull day in town and make it sound like the Battle of Waterloo. The Texan applies this ennobling talent to all things Texan. Most famous Texans were big men, and they grow a little bit every time anybody tells about them.

Yes, the Texan is a noble creature, fond of his mother,

small children, and oil leases. It is too bad there are not enough of them to spare to other states.

About the time we put up Explorer, somebody asked Dr. Wernher von Braun whether our satellite was likely to crash into Sputnik II. He said it was unlikely because outer space is so large.

"It is even bigger than Texas," he said.

This is the kind of snide remark that takes a large, Texas-type mind to overlook. After all, no missile fired off in Texas has ever failed yet. There are questions here to be solved more important than whether outer space is larger than Texas, about which Dr. von Braun regrettably is entitled to his opinion.

Who, for instance, is going along on the space ships?

A lot of us old World-War-II boys have already reached firm conclusions about this. From a bitter lesson, we know that it is better to be left behind with the pretty girls, the sirloin steaks, and the champagne while other men embark on hazardous odysseys. Also, the desire to wander in strange and faraway places has waned a great deal since everybody saw the TV ad showing that, no matter where you go, Mobilgas is already there.

I have personally granted the space people free access to my Navy health record, which shows that I am not physically fit for anything. I just don't think I can take Mars in my present state.

Probably there would be more enthusiasm for space travel if the people in charge of it were men of greater vision. They talk now of conquering outer space, when what is needed is a bold new approach. A bold man able to cut through the cobwebs of his mind, for instance, would suggest leapfrogging outer space and conquering what is beyond it. Being really bold, I have developed a new concept: Leapfrog space entirely. A man who can read German, French, Russian, and Einstein once told me that Dr. Einstein said that space is curvilinear. If you travel enough million light years, you will end up back in Texas.

That's where I was going in the first place.

THE FIRM CONCLUSIONS OF A
SEVERAL-MINDED MAN

After trying the thing out thoroughly, I have some mis-givings about the one-way streets that Dallas set up down-town. The one-way-street system places a very harsh burden on the average man. It requires him to know whether he is going or coming.

In practice the average man has seldom had to decide. America was built on different traditions. The ordinary pioneer, for instance, seldom knew whether he was com-ing or going and usually didn't give a hoot because there wasn't anything at either end of the trip. America actu-ally started on the moral downgrade when people began to fancy that they knew whether they were coming or going. As soon as men decided they knew where they were going, somebody built a saloon there.

The evidence clearly shows that even Columbus didn't know the answer to the question. The reports from those days are pretty sketchy and don't contain any good quotes, but midway in the voyage some of the seamen began to have their doubts. They went to Columbus and asked him whether they were going or coming.

"Sail on," he said, according to one reliable source. This patently was evading the question.

To a person reared in the good old American tradition, one-way streets solve nothing. It is all very well for the city to tell us to go east on Commerce and west on Elm. As a matter of practice, I have discovered that when I am on Commerce, I want to go west, not east. When I am on Elm, my destination is always east, not west. There is something unfunctional here.

A great many people seem to think one-way, and one-way streets may be a natural thing for them. For myself, I have always thought two ways about any subject that comes up. I belong to that splinter of the human race which deeply suspects a man who prefaces his remarks with "There's just no two ways about it." Automatically I start thinking that there is probably a parallel back alley or exit road which runs counter to the man's ideas.

At the edge of the fastest current there is always a backwash. Some few of us prefer to drift slowly with this against the stream, equipped with a piece of driftwood for protection against those who are shooting the rapids toward destiny.

You may ask what all this has to do with this bunch of traffic tickets on my desk, but I am going to think two ways about that, too, before answering.

One-way streets do make it possible for a man to get home fast. On the other hand, they make it almost impossible for him to get to work slow, so there may be no net gain.

The new system is in harmony with the political philos-

ophy of the times, of course. For the first time a place is
provided for the thousands of drivers who lean neither
to the left nor the right but stick to the middle of the
road.

A constitutionally querulous gentleman recently demanded to know what has become of the Angles and
Saxons around here. You hear no more about them, he
said, than you do of the Medes and the Persians.

It is a good question, deserving of an answer, and I am
luckily an expert on the subject. I have long felt that the
Anglo-Saxon is disappearing into the twilight because he
is an anachronism. He no longer fits in the world. The
Anglo-Saxon found his natural destiny as a marauder, a
looter. He does not civilize well. Other peoples master
better the mechanics and great pleasures of city living,
the tactics of the limited cold war that is commerce, and
the business of getting ahead in the arts.

The Anglo-Saxon languishes in such air. He used to be
known as Ethelred the Terrible. He has been known in the
last century as John Halifax, Gentleman, and then as
H. M. Pullham, Esq. This is a measure of his fall.

All these centuries of Anglo-Saxon ascendancy, if you
count the mixed Anglo-Saxons, have been years of marauding. The strangers who called on the British Isles, whether
Danes or Normans, were less interested in creating their
own luxuries than in making use of someone else's.

After the field for simple marauding gave out, there
remained the Spanish gold ships and, after that, colonies.

It must not be thought that the marauder was a useless thug. He had very great social uses. The Anglo-Saxon, for instance, was wonderful for civilizing the North American continent, if you mean by "civilizing" the killing of everything that opposed him and the destruction of any tree that he came across. It is the job of a marauder to civilize a place and turn over to the inheritors a one-touchdown lead to protect.

It must not be thought either that the marauder was inhumane. The Anglo-Saxon (and you can include some of us Americans) in later years was always willing to be known as a kindly man, a pukka sahib, so long as the natives did not become restless. It was only when he stopped trying to gain ground at somebody else's expense and started trying to protect his one-touchdown lead that he found other peoples were smarter.

Of course, the Anglo-Saxon was not the only marauder in history, and the practice has not died out yet. To name a few, there were the Medes and the Persians, the Huns, the Mongols, the followers of Mohammed, the Turks, and even the Romans.

What is the business of Empire anyway? It is the business of moving the pitiful baggage that humanity has been able to accumulate here in the twilight of eternity from one continent to another.

It is going on now. The wheel of Empire turns slowly but somewhere hits full swing. As the coaches say, you have to pick a hungry team as the winner, and I'd pick the Mongols for the next one. It would be nice to pick the

Romans, but darn it, our Italian friends have ruined themselves on pizza pie and easy living—and ruined us Angles and Saxons, too.

An Englishwoman touched on all this once in a letter to the London *Times:*

"Sir,—Is it not likely that the London pigeon will dominate the American eagle?

"I have the honour to be, Sir, your obedient servant, HELEN REID, Farm Cottage, Greenacre, Besham, Sussex."

The West Texas admirer of the golden eagle who mailed in this clipping was outraged and incoherent, but unfortunately the English lady is clairvoyant. The English are already known as a race of sitting pigeons, and the Americans are fast attaining this reputation among the peoples of the earth.

The two nations may have shone as predators, but now that they have turned meek and mild they will soon find themselves caught between the double crusts of a pie.

If you doubt that we give our custom to the pigeon rather than the eagle, look around and see how many eagles are being fed by people on the streets.

We profess to admire the eagle and we have made him our national bird, but we organize all our engines of science to seek him out and destroy him.

Meanwhile, we subconsciously glorify the pigeon. There is reason for this. The pigeon represents what we subconsciously wish to become. The pigeon lives by gifts for which he doesn't have to thank anybody. He is not re-

quired to clean up any messes he may make. He is willing
to allow superior authority to run everything so long as
feeding time is always remembered and plenty of free
housing is furnished.

The pigeon has a gray feathered suit.

The eagle, on the other hand, lives on danger. He is
likely to fight back at superior authority. He takes what
he wants and is therefore subconsciously hated by modern
man, who has acquired an inferiority complex because he
is unable to understand electricity.

If an eagle appeared in modern industry tomorrow, he
couldn't get a job.

In West Texas they are killing out the golden eagle on
the pretext of protecting a few spineless lambs, and this
is a tipoff. Man has always said he admired animals that
were brave and strong and fierce, but actually man
doesn't, because at his core he is a coward. He is cunning,
smart, and shrewd, but a coward, and he cannot stand
nobler beasts.

This may be the reason West Texas looks so barren.
Man has cunningly killed off all but the slavish animals
everywhere. In West Texas there were no slavish animals.
It was a land of fang and claw, of badger, rattlesnake,
tarantula, and wolf. Here man killed out a fauna.

The inflated dollar recently became a matter of police
record in Dallas.

Somebody at the police station took a robbery complaint
and listed the value of the stolen property as follows: "1

Wrist Watch, $10. 1 Billfold, $1. 1 $20 bill, $10." This last item showed signs of having been changed hurriedly, but probably it shouldn't have been.

Policemen are all too familiar with the exaggerated value most people put on their possessions and sometimes they are inclined to undervalue the goods. It makes the theft record look a lot better when the figures are all totaled up. Three or four years ago, the police records set the value of a stolen Stradivarius at two dollars. Ed Miley, a Dallas photographer, once lost an expensively rigged Speed Graphic camera to a thief. He was pretty burned up when he read the complaint sheet and found it listed as "1 Kodak, $5."

The value put on the twenty-dollar bill was probably about right, though. Certainly a twenty-dollar bill isn't worth more than $10 ordinarily.

Money seems to depreciate. It is highly valuable when it comes in the paycheck, but by the time you have rushed over to a creditor, it isn't worth much. You have probably noticed yourself that hard money is the kind you have to get, and soft money is the kind you have on hand when you have to pay bills.

I have observed a lot of other people in the same hock shop lately. At Corsicana, a man parked a new Cadillac Eldorado with an out-of-town license tag in front of the Levermann Paint Store. He got out of the car and started plugging one coin after another in the parking meter.

"There isn't any extra charge for parking a Cadillac," a native told him.

The driver laughed.

"I only dropped ten pennies in," he said. "Pennies are just about the only kind of money I have now."

The country would probably go back to debtor's prisons if it could afford to feed all the prisoners.

An Oak Cliff woman wrote this week asking advice on how to make $350 a month take care of $410 worth of bills. I have had a lot of experience at trying to do this, but I haven't quite figured it out yet.

The only advice I can give people about money is to quit using the stuff. Be a man. Get off the habit. Money has caused more family quarrels, more heartaches, and more broken homes than alcohol and other women put together, and many a young man has ruined his life by drifting into the money habit and then finding his supply cut off.

A Chicago sociologist not long ago classified all jobs from *one* to *seven* in the order of their difficulty and importance.

Everybody knew without even looking, of course, that the most difficult of all jobs and the least appreciated is that of sociologist.

As with all classifying systems, some of the Chicago man's cards got into the wrong pigeonholes. Right up there with sociologists and captains of industry in the most difficult jobs he has classified fleet admirals. Maybe so. I worked for one once, though, and he didn't have half as difficult a job being fleet admiral as I did being an ensign. Fair is fair. Let us give credit for being difficult where it is due.

The sociologist thinks that some college professors have

difficult jobs. Any college professor who thinks he is having a difficult time teaching physics, however, ought to
watch some of us try to learn it.

I personally was classifying and avoiding difficult jobs
before sociology ever got into the field, and I looked in
vain in the Chicago man's list for the most difficult of all
professions. Unloading barbed wire, or bob wire as it was
called in our country, is the most difficult of all jobs by far
because you have to take hold of it, but you had better
not.

Barbed wire comes in spools. Each spool weighs seventy
or eighty pounds, by guess. In lifting a spool, you have to
hold it away from the body unless you don't mind unloading part of yourself with the barbed wire. You cannot
hold the spool in your hand. The barbs make tatters out of
the toughest leather gloves. You lift the spool by inserting
your fingers in the holes in each end, and you balance the
seventy or eighty pounds on your fingers as you carry it out
of the freight car.

Being a fleet admiral or a captain of industry doesn't
have anything to do with it. Unloading barbed wire is just
as difficult for an illiterate as it is for them, though, being
big shots, they might get all the credit.

Some authorities hold that the second most difficult profession is that of unloading sand with a scoop shovel. However, this job is demanding rather than difficult.

The second most difficult job is carrying gypsum wall
board. The plaster board comes in slabs which are three to
four feet wide and eight to ten feet long. If you drop one,
it breaks, and you get to pay for it out of the day's salary.

Each board of this material is covered with plaster dust so slick that if you grasp the edge, the board will zip out of your hand. You can put a man at each end of the board, and they lift it on their fingertips.

So difficult are these jobs that if you ever get caught in one of them, you'll find it difficult to find anybody to accept your resignation. No fleet admiral or sociologist ever had any trouble quitting.

I went downtown to watch the last Armed Forces Day parade and noticed that the modern generation of military man isn't any better at keeping the ranks dressed while marching that I was fifteen years ago. Some strange kind of friction works on a squad of men marching abreast so that the left end of the line can never quite keep up. I quit trying to figure it out years ago.

I also spotted all the old types of military physique, shown off by those pitiless uniforms. There was the big-bellied, big-chested type who cannot mark time without having his hips work up and down in a kind of rotary motion. There was the thin, hollow-chested type who looks like a walking parenthesis even when his shoulders are rigidly squared. There was the swayback type who, even while standing at attention, looks as if he is about to butt somebody with his stomach. And there was the man with the fat, apple-cheeked face who was trying to look grim and succeeded only in looking pained. Through the two wars that I have known about, this has been the look of the best fighting men since Caesar's legions. They can handle any number of uniformed Adonises. Possibly they

are angered by any man who can look exactly right in
military dress.

Someone has kindly mailed in a copy of a book on auto
courtesy by Emily Post called *Motor Manners*. I was interested in such statements as "An honorable man or
woman would no more cheat traffic regulations than cheat
at games or in sports." This proves that Miss Post's heart
was in the right place but that she didn't get around much.
The old girl had got her peas on her knife. Honorable men
and women absolutely *would* cheat traffic regulations.
They do it all the time. Furthermore, sports and honor are
in different fields of endeavor these days.

Miss Post would have done well to stick to her field
with such instructions as "Do not eat scallops with your
gear-shift lever," and leave autos to us experts. Driving is
a field where courtesy should be tempered to the shorn
fender. What is too courteous for some sixty-year-old
shrimp may not be half courteous enough for a 250-pound
truck driver.

Miss Post said: "A courteous lady will not scold others
with her automobile horn any more than she would act like
a fishwife at a party." This begs the whole question of
whether the lady wouldn't act like a fishwife late in the
party. Miss Post also wrote: "The kind of vehicle a person
drives is not important." She was entitled to her opinion,
but it is probably not commonly held in Dallas.

On the whole, you'd have to say Miss Post was unsound
even if her book is scattered around by the Citizens Traffic Commission. The one thing I learned from her is that
the driver who darts into the space in which you are trying

to park is "impudent." This is not what most of us call him down here.

It is easy to think of a dozen more practical traffic rules than Miss Post's. For instance:

Do not drive when you have got yourself blind.

When you are rolling along in an MG and suddenly discover the front fender of a Chrysler Imperial hovering over your shoulder, never mind the traffic light.

When someone wants to race you from a standing stop, bend quickly forward over your steering wheel and glare at the road. This will fake him into racing off, and he will be out of your way.

Most people have their pet traffic peeves. Mine are drivers who weave in traffic, those who won't keep a proper interval between cars, and those with better-looking automobiles.

As an old expert, I have noticed that the most arrogant drivers navigate Cadillacs. They aren't bad drivers or intentionally discourteous. A Cadillac just comes with something built into the steering wheel which makes the driver oblivious of the other cars around him. The most inexpert drivers have Buicks. There are a lot of fine drivers in Buicks, but some others don't seem to do much except settle down at an intersection and make their engines go "*Whoom! Whoom!*"

I admire both Cadillac and Buick cars, and if I had either instead of a beat-up heap I could crowd nine-tenths of these drivers off the road.

One thing that is bound to distress the thinking man about the age we live in is that its liars are incompetent.

The competent liar is necessary to the political health of a people. Cynics may berate the liar in politics, but those of us who are truly sincere do not. After all, the liar lays the hard bedrock of myth upon which men base their lives. If a man believes in States' Rights or The Noble Savage or The Dictatorship of the Proletariat, he can go ahead and operate. Without this firm foundation of essential meaning that does not exist, the actions of his life seem quite pointless.

The liar who is gifted as well as competent is able to shape the myth into something his people may have dreamed they could be. Addressing a seedy, second-rate nation that then wore only the frayed tweeds of its former garment of greatness, Winston Churchill was able to persuade it that its people were Elizabethan corsairs. As a result, every woebegone five-foot Limey began acting like Sir Francis Drake.

By this kind of service, the competent liar has been able to cast man in a nobler mold than he has any right to assume.

The competent liar faces two problems. He must first persuade the people he is talking to that what he says is true.

In addition, however, he must take care that he himself never comes to believe what he says. This kind of lying takes an uncommonly honest man.

Not since F.D.R. have we had such a politician. It is doubtful that he believed absolutely everything he said; but certainly most of us did, and in trying to act out the role he had cast for us we were able to feel even a little noble. Since then, officeholders from constable on up have reversed the principle. They themselves have earnestly believed what they were saying while their listeners didn't.

The best that you can say for such a man is "Boy, is he sincere!"

This is no qualification for leading people.

Watching a Met performance of *La Traviata* one night, I discovered what was wrong with baseball. They have taken the opera out of it.

Like opera, baseball is a thing where the tightly knit dramatic passages come in short takes. There are frequent moments when all the players are just arranged around the stage. Nothing is happening. These moments all but demand that a performer take the center of the stage for a short bravura passage or a solo performance of some kind. They are set up for a Casey Stengel to lift his hat to the crowd and release the sparrow beneath it. A good manager who will lie down on home plate in front of the umpire and refuse to move, like Bobby Bragan, is invaluable.

These make the memorable moments in baseball.

In the old days of Snipe Conley and his crowd, you got a lot of fine arias even in the Texas League, but baseball has fallen into the hands of the stuffed shirts. A baseball scout now doesn't bother himself about whether a player can please a crowd. All he is interested in is whether the man can play baseball.

The result is what might be called the Mickey Mantle era. Mantle is a coolly efficient baseball perfectionist. His play is a joy for the *aficionados* to watch, but unfortunately they don't fill the grandstands, much less the bleachers. If you've seen a dozen Mantle games, you've seen them all. He will either hit or he won't; he'll make the catch or he won't. The law of accidents says this style of play will produce its great moments, but what was left in between except the sight of old Case striding toward the pitcher's mound like Father Time with a bill he means to collect? And now he is gone.

The baseball fan's consummate player was Babe Ruth. He could make striking out a thing that left people breathless for five minutes. First there was the fateful wait while the pitcher thought, or whatever they do out there. Then the nasty flicker of the bat over Ruth's shoulder which signified that he was about to strike. After that the long wait while Ruth wound his arms and legs round and round and possibly toppled over. If Ruth hit one, it was a hit that had everybody on their feet. If he struck out, you had the weak feeling of disaster narrowly averted.

A few people like Ted Williams have tried to save the national game. Yet, every time Williams shoots off his mouth, he is lectured by sports writers, who never could play right field on a sandlot team, about being a good sport. Better two thousand people in the stands who hate Williams' insides than two who say "Good boy."

A baseball scout who finds a promising player ought first to ask him "Have you ever wrestled?" If the answer is "Yes," the player ought to be signed up in a hurry on the theory that he has a yearning for acting and the taste for low humor that has marked most of the crowds' athletic favorites since the Romans got rid of that stuffed shirt Augustus.

For some time Shelby Friedman, the Forest Avenue pharmacist, owned a white rabbit named Harvey, a boon pal of his dachshund and his fox terrier.

One day he discovered that a workman had left a backyard gate open and Harvey was gone. Shelby made the rounds of the neighbors, and they all promised to telephone him if a white rabbit showed up. He then got a club and proceeded to beat through the bushes of a wooded area at the rear of his house on Hutchins Road in Oak Cliff.

He stirred out some cottontails but not Harvey. He emerged from the woods, which had heavy underbrush, rather ragged and bleeding from a dozen lacerations. He came out where an apartment project was going up, and a couple of carpenters were eying him as he stood there with staff and wounds.

He distinctly heard one of them say "Here comes Nature Boy."

This aroused Friedman to the realization that he must make strenuous efforts, such as putting a want-ad in The Dallas *News*. The *News* ad got immediate answers, as always, one from a woman on Glenhaven and another from a street off Worth, both miles and a broad river away. It didn't seem likely that Harvey could have got to either place, but Friedman went out to the house on Glenhaven. His wife immediately pointed out that the Glenhaven rabbit's ears were not as long or as broad as Harvey's, but the woman who had found him was disposed to argue.

"It must be him," she said. "I don't have any place to keep him."

So Friedman took the rabbit home and dropped him in with the dogs who were supposed to be his friends. Sure enough, the rabbit took off at jet speed and left a hole in what was supposed to be a rabbitproof fence.

There were now two lost white rabbits, and the one in the Worth Street neighborhood turned out to be a Harriet, not a Harvey.

Just then Mr. and Mrs. Harry E. Kelley, a block away, found an extra white rabbit among the ones they raise. Mrs. C. E. Witt, who knew the Friedmans, was visiting the Kelleys and had seen Friedman's ad. She mentioned it and the Kelleys started action. Friedman had a faint suspicion that this was the second white rabbit, but he tried. He got the rabbit and dropped it among his dogs. Sure enough, the rabbit took off for the hole he thought he had left in the fence. This time Friedman had bolstered his defenses, and the rabbit failed to gain at the fence. While he was still stunned, Friedman returned him.

By then Mrs. Witt had received a call from a young bachelor in the neighborhood. Had anyone lost a rabbit? He had, without a drink, found one on his doorstep.

Friedman took off immediately. He found the young man and discovered that he had given the rabbit to a friend of his girl friend. The young man mentioned that the rabbit probably by now had been Sunday dinner.

Aghast, Friedman flew off and located the girl. Harvey turned out to be still alive in the cage; put back with the dogs, he was content. Friedman was thankful. If he hadn't got the other rabbit from miles away, he might never have set up the contacts that located the one close by.

In an owner-rabbit relationship like this, you wonder who has the upper hand.

Any serious-minded person is bound to be alarmed these days by the decline in the quality of Dallas panhandlers. Their imaginations have dried up. A couple of them, both obviously in a bad state of postalcoholic shock, hit me up at the corner of Record and Jackson on a recent day. The best story that the two of them could offer was that one of them needed only twenty-five cents to finish buying a bus ticket to Texarkana to be at the bedside of an ailing sister. I refuse to buy such sorry fiction. You can read better stuff in the magazines any time.

Back before the war, nightfall used to be the signal for dozens of tattered men to hit the downtown in the Lamar Street neighborhood. They could give you an arresting excuse for a handout and then a romantic story of past glories well worth the quarter. One ancient man, leering from under bushy brows, once told me he needed the money to telegraph his daughter congratulations on the birth of his latest grandchild. Another explained that he had learned how to loot a penny slot machine with one coin and a knife blade and needed only capital to start his new venture. He then hiccuped and said, "Pardon me, friend. I can't hit the ground with my hat."

One old beggar used to ask for his handout with a tin cup, though he wasn't blind. If you didn't have pocket change, you could satisfy him by pouring him something out of a bottle.

These panhandlers were all broken-down old men, driftwood of the financial tidal wave that hit us before Roosevelt. They lived in second-story flophouses above the cheap business places of the neighborhood, dirty, shadowy, cobwebby barracks with rows of cots along the barren floor and a custodian who sat at a table by the door with a cigar box before him for a cash register. Lodging in the best of these cost twenty-five cents a night. A dozen hole-in-the-wall cafés catered to the tattered man. For eight cents he could get breakfast, two eggs, bacon, and coffee. His lunch—meat, three vegetables, a dab of dessert, and drink—cost fifteen cents. His seven-course dinner at night cost a quarter, and it was food he could eat, too. He could take a streetcar to the residential areas and beg enough old clothing to make out. In this way a lot of the old panhandlers finished out their lives.

In all my palavering with aged panhandlers, I never found an ordinary man. Everybody in his day had been somebody. The old men would stand on the street corner for a long time after you had coughed up your bit, telling of the money they used to make and the people they had bossed, or maybe about the time they had made the run to the Klondike.

In the Thirties, all those stories could have been true, of course. You were inclined to doubt them mainly because some of the old men liked to change past careers every three or four weeks.

Most of them cadged money for drinks unabashedly, but they cadged money for everything else, too. One bitterly discouraged old man confronted a newspaper confrere of mine one night and explained that he needed a dime to finish out his sleeping money. The newspaperman refused but offered to buy a beer. The old man insisted that he only wanted a dime for a bed.

"Well, here's a dime to sleep on. And here's a quarter. Go buy yourself a beer."

"Damn it," said the old man. "I don't want a beer. Take back your goddam quarter." He thrust it back but held on to the dime and went his way.

They seem better in retrospect than the derelicts who now beg money to buy cheap wine and then slip off under the viaduct to drink it with goof balls. These modern panhandlers ought to be ashamed of taking money they haven't earned.

The outsider who visits our part of Texas is bound to wonder why men who drive Cadillacs in Dallas always wear big, farmer-type straw hats.

I once knew a West Texas cowman who had an explanation for why cowboys on scrawny range ponies often wore fancy boots, spectacular hats, and spangled chaps. "He's trying to disguise the horse," the rancher would say. It is pretty hard to disguise a Cadillac even with a very big straw hat. The explanation of this phenomenon lies elsewhere.

It seems to me that the hayseed hat in the Cadillac may be a straw in the wind, an indication that we are really coming into the Age of the Common Man. It may be an expression of an unconscious human yearning toward the realization of the American dream.

I am different. If I owned a Cadillac, I would want one of those gigantic Stetsons with fur on it that you comb or else a great floppy panama like the Latin American dictators used to wear. These hats have the grandeur, the sweep, and the drama to go with the Cadillac.

To my mind the toniest car ever built was the Pierce Arrow of thirty or forty years ago, the one with the head-lamps in the fenders and the glass pane behind the front seat to keep the owner from being contaminated by the chauffeur.

The man who owned this car did not wear a common-man straw hat. He wore a derby or a homburg. He also wore a high, stiff white collar, high enough so that you could tell it was a collar and distinguished from the ordinary man's by being of cloth that had to be laundered instead of celluloid. He wore a black alpaca coat and carried a cane.

He did not wear a dollar sign on his shirt the way the cartoonists drew him, but he tried his best to dress like what the people of our country called "one of them eastern magnates." The word *tycoon* had not been invented, so every one of them was a magnate and belonged to a conspiracy called Wall Street.

Having been born below the aristocracy, I believe in aristocrats. They have responsibilities to the rest of us.

As an admirer of the unrestrained aristocrat, I would call upon our Cadillac friends to doff their farmer straws and pick up their responsibilities to the rest of us except for one thing.

The straw hat in the Cadillac is unfortunately more in the American tradition than the aristocrat in the Cadillac.

The straw hat seems to be saying "Here I have all this money, but I am really just an old country boy." This is probably true, but before the old country boy was able to get out of the country he wanted to throw away the farmer straw and get a Stetson with fur on it that he could comb.

Nevertheless, his straw hat is a symbol of a noble impulse. It may lead in the years ahead to nothing but the best of the Cadillacs for every common man, and we shall all march arm and arm together in the Straw-hat Brotherhood.

The people who opened up the new toll road between Fort Worth and Dallas could have saved themselves a lot of trouble if they had clearly settled one important question before they opened it. The question is *Where does it lead?* Dallas or Fort Worth?

Any right-thinking, intelligent person knows, of course, that the toll road leads from Fort Worth to Dallas; but you would be surprised how many people can't tell which way a road is going. Take that city slicker who years ago braked his car to a stop in front of Mr. J. I. Case Jones' implement shop out in West Texas and yelled to Mr. Jones from the car window.

"Say, friend," he asked, "where does this road lead to?"

"Why," Mr. Jones told him, "it leads to here, of course."

For a long time after that Mr. Jones used the story to illustrate the common kind of raising that city people get.

"Looked like he got mad at me just because I done him a favor," he said.

Just because a person knows where a road is on the map or knows which town it goes through doesn't mean that he knows where the road is going. One day the youngest Larkin kid out in the Lariat country came home in high excitement from his first taste of geography. The teacher, Miss Weems, had said you could start out and walk right around the world. If you walked west down the road and kept on, said the youngster, you would eventually come from the east right back where you started.

The kid's dad, Jubal Larkin, shook his head at that and said it just wasn't so.

"The road forks at Portales," he explained.

Egghead people are always getting the way a road really is mixed up with what they think a road ought to do. My dad once knew an Ozark old-timer who told a stranger, when asked where one of those mountain roads went, that it didn't go anywhere.

Why, then, asked the smart aleck, was the road there in the first place.

"Because," the old-timer explained patiently, "it follows the creek bottom."

Americans started losing their self-reliance the minute they began to believe that a place is more important in geography than a person.

We are told that the mountain men could roam the whole of the vast, unsettled West without becoming lost; in a way, they could. They might not know where St. Louis was, or Bent's Fort or the Missouri River, but they knew for a certainty that they personally were right there in that little old canyon or on top of that hill or wherever they were. As long as a man knows where he is, he can find a place that is temporarily lost, but if he doesn't know where he is, it doesn't do any good to know where places are located.

An old rancher who used to ship cattle to Kansas City every year summed it up once. He always sent two or three men along with the cattle train, but he announced that he himself was never going to Kansas City.

Said he: "It's at least seven hundred miles from here, away to God out in nowhere."

There are areas in life where our ordinary ideas of progress simply don't measure up. In some things, the only way to get ahead of the game is to retreat gracefully. The idea is to make haste slowly. Take age, for instance.

An encouraging note on this score is sounded by the life-insurance people, who claim that a woman who is thirty years old these days is only twenty-seven.

This may be true statistically over the nation, but it is not true of Texas women. A Texas woman who is thirty years old is actually only twenty-five. I know as well how to please a woman as the insurance industry. Butter won't melt in *my* mouth either.

As a matter of fact, this idea illustrates a decided trend that is developing in modern thought. In defense matters, for instance, two hundred men with Colt .45 pistols are stronger than two thousand men with Colt .45 pistols if you reorganize the Defense Department.

If you write a poem called "Howl" that doesn't seem to say anything, it is actually fraught with meaning, really fraught. A football player who runs the hundred-yard dash in 11 seconds actually runs it in 9.6 by the time they start writing about him on the All-America squad.

Black is really white. It just has some impurities in it.

As an old-fashioned type, all I know now is that a newspaper columnist who is eighty-one years old is actually eighty-one years old. The insurance industry doesn't even think enough of him to butter him up.

For a long time some of us cherished the notion that the newspaper itself belonged to the old-fashioned world where things were finite, hard, immutable, and true in a way that most people have forgotten.

"One thing about it," I argued recently. "The newspaper column is always 13 ems wide."

"Oh, no it isn't. It's 11.3," declared our expert. "That is, it is 11.3 before it is shrunk."

It was a shock. When a shrunk 11.3 equals a 13, it is time to give up numeration instead of sanity.

Time and again I have discovered that Isaac Newton is easier to understand than Einstein. When I was growing up, all the physicists were fond of revealing that meter sticks were not exactly a meter long. Now the attitude is "What the devil? Who cares? Will it orbit?"

Any wise man will have to go along with saying that Texas women of thirty are really only twenty-five, however. Except for the one who is a member of our family. She is only twenty-one.

I made an early-autumn visit a year or two ago to Aspen, Colorado. It is full of plain, ancient houses with

wooden gingerbread around the porch columns and slick
new European-looking meeting places for the skiing pro-
fessionals. It has a couple of graying, deserted mines on
the hillsides above it and claims the world's largest ski
lift. Along this ski lift, where you dangle in a chair twenty
to a hundred feet above the ground, there are signs saying that anybody who jumps off the lift will not be allowed
to ride it again; and when we were there, the proprietor,
with apparent disregard for what it might do to his
business, was passing out along with his own leaflets another by the Colorado Bar Association on why you ought
to make a will.

Old-timers who remember the mining days were shooting the breeze along the town's sidewalks, and an attractive little blonde with the Vassar look was running a place
called The General Store.

Aspen is a fine, objective place from which to think upon
this land which lives with history. The days seem to stretch
back before the eyes to the time that De Vargas stood in
Santa Fe plaza almost three hundred years ago.

It has been written that these Spanish captains of men
were driven to take this country by a greed for gold and
souls, but this was said mostly by historians with no knowledge of what moved such men. Take Francisco Coronado
—or Corinado, as a Trinidad hotelkeeper prefers to call
him. Coronada probably took his jaunt into the West to get
away from family responsibilities and perhaps partly for
the fine feeling of soldiering, the satisfactions of command
far from the senile interference of a viceroy, the smell
of saddle leather, and the smell of pine in the campfires.

This land would have called such men even if it had had no gold. Destiny seems to do its unhurried brooding at the foot of these pink-and-blue peaks. The vastness draws the human being on even as it reduces him to puniness, like a glimpse into the stars. It is a strangely beautiful land with a ghastliness also about it, for the barren sides of the Rockies and the deserts, scarred by water and wind, are a preview of the end of our human world.

At Aspen, the wind in the fall flows like gold in the autumn aspen leaves, and the mountains lift up around one like the human heart when it beholds them. You sense the shades of the lonely men who first trapped the beaver ponds thereabouts and located the mines.

On the day we sat down to do our thinking, some hundreds of people wearing Alpine shorts and knee-high hose, or auto racing costumes, gathered in the town to worry about how their entry would fare against a late-coming Ferrari. It was a day of sports-car racing with cars from all over the country—Allards, Jaguars by the dozen, a Mercedes.

Yes, the West has changed. A good two-thirds of these cars belonged to doctors who hunt their gold in a different way.

Gold is where you find it.

A friend of mine who is fond of TV westerns has suddenly decided they are unsanitary.

It seems that every one of these TV town marshals, once he has beaten ten badmen to the draw all in one split second, has the habit of walking dramatically away from the corpses and letting them lie. On a recent Sunday evening my friend counted sixteen desperados left dead on the street or in the desert or someplace.

He only catches the Sunday-night quota of desperados. This sort of thing is bound to go on every day of the week in those tough western towns, especially on Saturday night. My friend figures there must be thousands of these used, unburied desperados lying around over the landscape.

He is pretty sure this is a violation of the sanitary code.

The movies used to take a more public-spirited attitude. They did not leave their dead badmen around for the community to take care of. The least a movie sheriff ever did was bring back his desperado lashed over the back of a horse.

The higher type of movie sheriff buried his badman right before your eyes. After Mr. James Stewart had shot one of them, he always seemed to have a trenching shovel on the saddle behind his slicker. You would see a shot of Mr. Stewart digging in some rocky ground. Then you would see a mound of earth over the grave and Mr. Stewart's hands placing a cross made out of two sticks.

Mr. Stewart not only buried them; he took time, with a kind of "aw, shucks" offhandedness, to deliver a small speech about man's fate, the wrongheadedness of the deceased, and the general foolishness of having to kill twenty or thirty men a day.

If a highly paid, millionaire-type sheriff like Mr. Stewart can spare the time to dig a grave, a low-paid deputy like Chester ought to be able to keep them dug ahead of time.

TV proceeds on the false assumption, apparently, that

the people of the old West didn't like to bury a badman. This doesn't square with any records from that period. Actually, the people of the old West were only too glad to bury him; it was living with him that they dreaded.

This kind of foolishness is what we get for trying to have "adult" westerns. My friend says westerns never were adult, and if they get to be that way, they will lose all their adult viewers.

It is all the rage these days to castigate the violence on TV and the printed page that is supposed to be brutalizing our youngsters. Personally, I think all this uproar is totally unnecessary.

If you check your kid's comic books, you'll probably find the punks these days are getting a pretty watered-down product for their dime. If a man has to get killed to get Roy Rogers into action, he is shot without bloodstains on his clothes. Mostly the villains just hit their victims over the head without sound effects and tie them up without harming them.

This is all pretty pale beside that same Young Wild West I used to read locked up in my room in an Ozark log house, the room with its own personal sapling growing up through a knothole in the floor. In one action, for instance, Young Wild West's sweetheart, Arietta, had been captured by the Indians and tied to the stake. They were dancing about her and fixing to burn her alive when our hero and his pal, Buckskin Charley, arrived. With an unearthly cry, Buckskin Charley charged. He buried a tomahawk to the handle in one Indian's head. He cut another's throat. Frothy blood gushed and soaked the ground.

This was writing to raise the hair on the head and cause the blood to curdle. Adults have a tendency to forget how much fun it was about the time they cease having any hair on the head to rise or blood to curdle.

For the ultimate in violence and gore for children, you have to go to the great classics of children's literature. You could argue that the bloodiest scene in them was in that chapter of *Treasure Island* where Jim Hawkins returned to find the schooner a ship of murdered men. If you read this chapter when you were seven, you will never forget how Israel Hand, with that dirk in his teeth, chased young Hawkins up the rigging and, hurling the dirk, pinned his shoulder to the mast. To me this scene produced more fright than the father of Hansel and Gretel, who took his children into the woods to kill them as if they were whelps, or the poisonings and cleaner murders of Grimm's fairy tales.

In his older years a boy will read *Macbeth* and find that it is bloodier than Young Wild West, for a fair section of the world's great literature deals with murder, bloodletting, and mortal intrigue. A lot of magazines wouldn't be cutting back on the budget if they would get back to this meat and bread of fiction. The heart of any man's morality is what he will commit violence for.

Dr. James B. Conant, the Harvard man, came down to Dallas to deliver his speech on beefing up the American schools. He said schools ought to be consolidated until no high school turned out fewer than one hundred graduates, the idea being that the high schools would then have faculties, laboratories, and libraries large enough to teach the needed subjects.

Dr. Conant is undoubtedly a very smart man, but some of us would like just once to see him consolidate the schools of Van Horn, Texas, population fifteen hundred or maybe eighteen hundred.

It took a lot of ruthless consolidation just to make the town of Van Horn, Culberson County, appear in sight on the highway. Culberson is a county roughly the size of Delaware. It is as large as Dallas, Tarrant, Denton, and Collin counties put together and contains almost as much vacant land as the city limits of Houston. Take all the people in this great, gaunt land and cram them into an area one building deep along the highway, and you have Van Horn.

Culberson County has 666 kids of school age. This looks like a ranch brand, and somebody may have got hold of the wrong tally sheet; but it is roughly one hundred miles to anybody with whom they can be consolidated.

Van Horn is in desert country. I will get shot for saying this the next time I pass that town, but journalistic sophistry has its limits. It is the kind of raw-mountain, raw-grasslands country that breeds mystics and imaginative, lyrical chambers of commerce.

This is not to reflect on Van Horn. It happens to be located in the country that I think is the most beautiful on earth. I have never liked mountains covered with pines or other trees. Varmints hide behind trees, and if a man can't learn a lesson from Braddock's defeat, why study history? I prefer the Diablos of the Van Horn country on late afternoons when the darkly purple shadows hang in pleats around the carmine-tinted rocky peaks. Here is an infinite loneliness and an infinite freshness before your eyes. Men have been in this country a long time but they have never been able to handle it; on its ghastly peaks, its sun-colored pastures, and its shimmering salt flats are still visible the handprints of God.

Van Horn has other attractions. Television there was impossible for a while. It was thought that the pure, pollution-free air rebelled at it, but an enterpriser put a relay tower on a nearby peak a year or two ago, and now Van Horn youngsters have as little time to study as they do anywhere else. Van Horn has an excellent little hotel and is liberally lighted with neon signs. A local story tells of a visitor who put up at the hotel at night and looked out his window. Next morning he looked out the window again when the signs were off and exclaimed: "My God, what did they do with the town?"

Also, it is only in the light of the semi-desert that the shimmer of sunlight on the dancing leaves of cottonwoods and poplars has the feel of a New England spring.

Dr. Conant would do well to spend some time at the Van Horn hotel and watch the shadow cross the land. He has been too long in the centers of population and computing machines.

The Van Horns of this earth are scattered over more than two-thirds of its land mass. Of even those parts of the earth's surface which can support man, most is semi-desert, and the semi-desert's voice says "Where you cannot expand, contract."

Does Dr. Conant wish a knowledge of languages? Van

Horn is border country, and the people who have grown up there have been bilingual from the time they could speak.

I grew up in such a small high school. Sixteen courses were needed for graduation, and the school offered eighteen. The one laboratory course was physics, and you passed physics or else. You got the four years of English that he wants and also four years of math. There were a few courses like history. The faculty wasn't large, but with eight or ten students in a class, the English teacher had time to teach English.

It is true that few of her students now could parse one of Thomas Wolfe's more exalted sentences, but it would be fun to see Dr. Conant try.

The influence of the military and strategic expert has been greatly enhanced by the coming of television. Both, it appears, are here to stay in increasing quantity and authority.

You know, of course, that military experts are not found in the armed services. They are found on newspapers and on the radio and TV, but these days they are mostly found in the State Department or the federal civil service. Generals and admirals can't cut the mustard as military experts. They are always letting the number of guns and men on hand influence their ideas. They are tradition-minded.

A military expert attempting to ply his trade in the military services is always being interrupted by a demand to know how much five-inch ammunition is on hand or who left the beer warehouse unlocked. Nobody can worry about high strategy if the door to the beer warehouse is open.

The true, or civilian, type of military expert is a very valuable man. He is the only man who can make war interesting. If he didn't come in on the radio or TV every day, the civilians would get just as bored with war as the soldier, sailor, or airman.

I once had the privilege of taking a minor part in a North Pacific military operation and hearing at the same time on the radio what some of the best military experts in the country thought about it. If I hadn't been listening, I would never have known how important and dangerous our operation was.

GIs went into an operation with all sorts of small booklets or mimeographed sheets or lectures to tell what it was all about, but they always liked a military expert to come in on the radio and make it more fascinating. It was always nice to hear that "Our troops are poised, bayonets fixed," especially when you were lying around on the ground, bored, with nothing to do at the moment.

It is evident from some recent TV performances that the military expert has now been burdened down with a new responsibility. He apparently has to take a simple operation and make it complex enough to understand.

Back during one of the Formosa crises, President Eisenhower made a speech about it. The President spoke in simple, direct language. Nearly everybody thought they had understood him until the expert came on right afterward to interpret the speech. After the expert got through, some of us stayed up most of the night trying to piece things together.

It was good that the expert was around. If he hadn't interpreted the whole speech, we would have thought we knew what was happening in foreign affairs.

Every day or so somebody in our set gets worried about how civilization will be destroyed by the hydrogen bomb. Personally, I have never bothered much about what the bomb is going to do to civilization, being more concerned about what it may do to me.

Anyhow, it is not in our family's nature to worry about such things. I was conditioned against it as a boy by several relatives, mainly Uncle Tuck. Uncle Tuck was an expert on cyclones, that being a time before the tornado had been invented. He visited the site of every cyclone he could, "to look at the remains," as he said. He read everything he could find about the cyclones that he could not visit.

Uncle Tuck had a theory that one day a he-horse of a cyclone half the world wide was going to come boiling up out of the Pacific Ocean, sweep around the earth and destroy civilization and Woodward, Oklahoma, besides.

"The sinners will be separated from the goats," he said.

Uncle Tuck was pretty cheerful about this prediction, however, and often said he hoped he would be around to see what happened.

Anybody who hasn't let recorded history blind him to what really happened knows that civilization has already been destroyed a number of times. Some expert recently wrote for the *Saturday Evening Post* a story about the great atmospheric inversion in prehistory which quick-froze great mammoths in an instant as they grazed and preserved them and their stomach contents whole to the present time in the Arctic. Once the Mayan people tended green fields all across this part of Texas.

I have been conditioned to doom, should it come. After my grandmother's descriptions of hellfire and brimstone, the H-bomb sounds rather gentle.

No, it's not the bomb that really worries me. It's what follows it. As I see it, after the bombs and missiles have wrecked our cities and factories, all that will be left is some of us people. Then suddenly the Russian soldiers appear.

It will do no good then to yell for the block warden and tell him to get these characters out of here. The block warden is unreliable. I know, being always too weak-minded to turn down one of those civic honors with a lot of work attached to it.

Considering the situation the other night, I came upon the answer: a citizenry trained in guerrilla tactics and in shootings. Such a force ought to bewilder anybody.

The idea, in brief, is a nationwide organization with each minute man equipped with a gun and proficient in its use. In case a man has to roam the countryside, this gun ought to be one for which he can get ammunition by smashing into a country hardware store. Smashing plate-glass windows ought to be a lot of fun, and nobody can be blamed for it if he is defending his country.

These men ought to be trained in things like basic radio

and the treatment of accidental gunshot wounds. They ought to know how to use dynamite; most people think it's good only for fishing.

The police will object to all this, probably, on the ground that guns in the hands of a lot of people are dangerous, but this is a silly objection.

After all, we live in dangerous times that demand desperate measures.

We are laying for Russians at our house.

It is for this reason that we insist that friends who call by night at the Crume manse stop before they enter the yard, step cautiously into the street, cup their hands and yell loudly "*Hello, the house!*" This is a fine old pioneer custom that I am starting up again.

After the visitor has heard us yell "*Hello*" in return, he is to yell back so that he can be heard about a quarter of a mile: "Call in your dogs."

There aren't any dogs at our house, but this is the way the thing was done by the pioneers, and it is best to follow protocol in such matters. After all, who is a better model for the American guerrilla of today than the American pioneer?

ABOUT THE AUTHOR

Paul Crume is a leading columnist with *The Dallas Morning News,* where his "Big D" receives front-page space. His newspaper career began when he was thirteen and printer's devil on the *State Line Tribune* in Farwell, Texas. A graduate of the University of Texas, he has been with *The Dallas Morning News* since 1936 (with four years out for wartime Navy service). His column has appeared since 1952 and enjoys an extensive following. Born in 1912 in the Ozarks near Alpena Pass, Arkansas, he spent his boyhood in West Texas, and now resides in, of course, Dallas.

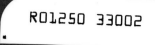